DATE DUE

AG 10			

DEMCO 38-296

Measuring the Employment Effects of Regulation

Measuring the Employment Effects of Regulation

Where Did the Jobs Go?

NEAL S. ZANK

Q

QUORUM BOOKS
Westport, Connecticut • London

Library of Congress Cataloging-in-Publication Data

Zank, Neal S.
    Measuring the employment effects of regulation : where did the
jobs go? / Neal S. Zank.
        p.   cm.
    Includes bibliographical references and index.
    ISBN 1–56720–070–2 (alk. paper)
    1. Industrial policy—United States.   2. Trade regulation—United
States.   3. Unemployment—United States.   4. Environmental policy—
United States.   5. United States.   National Commission for
Employment Policy.   Measuring employment effects in the regulatory
process.   I. Title.
    HD3616.U46Z36   1996
    331.13'7973—dc20   96–911

British Library Cataloguing in Publication Data is available.

Library of Congress Catalog Card Number: 96–911
ISBN: 1–56720–070–2

First published in 1996

Quorum Books, 88 Post Road West, Westport, CT 06881
An imprint of Greenwood Publishing Group, Inc.

Printed in the United States of America

The paper used in this book complies with the
Permanent Paper Standard issued by the National
Information Standards Organization (Z39.48–1984).

10 9 8 7 6 5 4 3 2 1

Contents

Preface

An increasing amount of attention has been focused in recent years on the employment effects of government regulation. Controversy over the implementation and impacts of government rules (such as the minimum wage, affirmative action, and Davis-Bacon) are now central to current public policy debates relating to employment and labor markets. The purpose of this book is to increase the public dialogue about how to improve consideration of employment impacts in the regulatory decision-making process.

In January 1993, the National Commission for Employment Policy published a study, *Measuring Employment Effects in the Regulatory Process: Recommendations and Background Study*, that examined the employment impacts of regulation. The commission was an independent federal agency authorized under the Job Training Partnership of 1982. Until its demise on September 30, 1995, the Commission for twenty-two years had analyzed employment and training issues and policies and made recommendations to the president and Congress in areas where policy or programmatic changes would assist the nation's work force in becoming more productively employed. The project director of the commission's study was Nancy A. Bord, visiting fellow, Manufacturers Alliance for Productivity and Innovation. The other members of the project team were John Addison, Glenn Harrison, and Eva Elisabet Rutstrom, all of the University of South Carolina.

Shortly after the commission's report was published, discussions between Nancy Bord and me led us to conclude that the subject of the report would be of interest to a broader population than those reached by the commission, especially if the information could be presented in a context that provided the reader with a useful background for understanding regulatory policy. That conclusion evolved into further discussions, which eventually resulted in this book. This book differs from the original commission report in three significant ways. It provides an expanded discussion of almost all areas in the original report, including the history of federal regulation of business and the role of the president and the judiciary in regulatory review. The book also presents an overview of the literature on the costs of regulation, both economywide and in individual labor market categories of rules; an historical view of the use of, and issues associated with, cost/benefit analysis in regulatory review; and an analysis on how federal regulatory agencies currently account for employment effects during the rulemaking process. Finally, I have attempted to remove or explain as much technical language as possible in the hope that the reader who does not have a technical background will be able to understand the issues that are raised and the possible solutions that are presented in this book.

It is hoped that this analysis will lead policymakers, legislators, regulatory analysts, and academics to pay greater attention to the issues of the employment effects of regulation. I also hope that students of the regulatory process; those with an interest in public policy, regulatory policy, and public administration; and analysts and experts in employment and labor policy will find that this book directs them down avenues of information and opens up lines of communication.

Acknowledgments

This book would not have been possible without the participation, assistance, and encouragement of many colleagues who were associated with both this book and the original report issued by the National Commission for Employment Policy. Although Nancy Bord was unable to participate in writing this book, I appreciate the initial advice that she provided on its structure and the comments that she provided on an early version of the manuscript. I would also like to thank William Laffer III and the project team at the University of South Carolina (John Addison, Glenn Harrison, and Eva Elisabet Rutstrom) for their diligence; some of their initial work was used to form the core of some of the chapters in this book as well as Appendices A and D.

I also appreciate the time and effort of Randall Lutter of the Office of Information and Regulatory Affairs of the Management and Budget, Executive Office of the President. His comments and suggestions challenged and helped frame some of the arguments presented in this book.

I would like to thank three people associated with the National Commission for Employment Policy for their support of the research that led to the original Commission report: John C. Gartland, former chairman; Donald Jones, a former commissioner; and Barbara McQuown, former director.

Finally, I want to thank my family for their support and encouragement in writing this book and in all of my literary efforts.

Of course, any errors presented in this volume are my responsibility.

Measuring the Employment Effects of Regulation

1

Introduction

Throughout our nation's history, business and society have had to deal with government regulation of the economy. There is no dispute that the involvement of government in the marketplace—regardless of the state's intentions—affects the economy in general and employment in particular. Differences appear when attempts are made to quantify the extent to which regulations adversely affect productivity by increasing costs and reducing output for a given level of inputs.

The time is ripe to reassess the role of the government and the private sector in economic growth and job creation. We saw the number of pages printed annually in *The Federal Register* increase to 69,608 pages in 1993 in President Clinton's first year in office, the third highest number of pages of all time. We have seen the number of federal regulators increase to 128,615 under President Clinton from 101,963 under President Reagan. Economists now estimate the cost of regulation on the economy to be between $400 and $500 billion, or from $4,000 to $5,000 per family (and that is above the dollars paid by taxpayers to fund regulatory agencies).

In addition, in the name of environmental protection and other social goals, government has ignored or ridden roughshod over property rights; federal bureaucrats and regulators have deprived many individuals and small businesses of the exclusive rights to use and derive income from their assets or resources in order to protect the "wetland" created in the previous week's rainstorm and to ensure the "rights" of snail darters, owls, and a whole host of animals. In the name of fair employment, we had to endure years of race norming. Under the total barrage of regulation, we have also seen scores of industrial facilities close throughout the nation and move their operations and employment opportunities.

Many jurisdictions—federal, state, and local—have erected ponderous, lengthy, and complex structures of rules and procedures that prevent entrepreneurs from investing and creating jobs. Time is money, and excessively long planning times impose a substantial cost that small-scale entrepreneurs lack the capital reserves to manage. These obstructions tend to reduce the quantity and quality of goods and services available to the economy, and thus hinder economic growth.

For years, government has regulated the prices of the goods or services provided in a particular industry, or the quantities sold, or other economic aspects of a specific industry or market, such as the number of firms in the industry or the freedom of firms to enter or leave the industry. This type of regulation has pernicious effects on private enterprises and economic growth. Regulation does not always succeed in ensuring the most efficient use of resources and the most economical range of services and products for consumers. In addition, many aspects of existing regulations (e.g., those dealing with telecommunications) have been rendered obsolete by new technologies.

Yet, at the heart of the regulatory debate is jobs. Does government regulation of the economy cause a decrease in employment levels and wage rates, or does regulation create new job opportunities in new fields? The answer to that question has given rise in recent years to a pair of related issues that have gained increasing attention: how the impacts of regulation on the economy and employment can be more accurately analyzed and measured, and whether some regulations that resulted in significant negative employment effects might have been prevented (i.e., amended to mitigate or eliminate the negative effects before being promulgated) if analyses of employment effects were included in regulatory decision making.

A government regulation has both negative and positive effects on employment patterns throughout the economy, effects that occur in response to new regulations or changes in existing regulations. Among the negative effects are limiting the number of new employees hired, dismissing some current employees, and lowering salaries. Businesses may close down or relocate facilities or operations because of the increased burden of regulation.

Proponents of these rules claim that the workplace is safer and fairer (in hiring and firing), and that companies accrue the benefits of lower medical and insurance costs. They also claim that the demands of regulatory compliance may sometimes create jobs (e.g., Equal Employment Opportunity coordinator) or even entire industries (e.g., pollution abatement equipment manufacturing). Whichever side one takes, these issues are central to much of the current public policy debate as it relates to employment and labor markets.

The relationship among regulation and labor, capital, and output is such that increased regulation lowers profitability, and that, in turn, reduces investment spending, which also lowers productivity, and that—in the long run—lowers living standards. If market forces were allowed to operate, the interaction of the demand for and the supply of any category of labor would determine both the amount of labor services actually bought and its price. For example, real wages (the wage rate as measured by the amount of goods and services that it can buy) will fall in markets where labor supply grows faster than labor demand.

However, both the level of employment and the wage rate are influenced by a variety of government policies that affect the demand for, and cost of, labor (as well as by a set of related issues that includes migration flows, the regional distribution of the population and labor force, and the distribution of income). These rules set wages above market clearing wage rates that do not reflect labor market demand and supply conditions, causing wages to rise more rapidly than productivity. This will generally benefit workers employed in relatively high-paying industries and firms at the expense of other workers, as well as the unemployed. Such laws push labor costs beyond the capacity of some firms.

Government regulations may artificially increase the relative cost of labor and indirectly stimulate the selection of capital-intensive production processes (in lieu of adopting labor-intensive methods). This means that less employment would be generated for the same level of economic activity that companies would otherwise use in the absence of regulation. The misallocation of resources caused by these distortions also reduces the production potential of the economy, giving rise to a further loss of employment. This is particularly true when capital goods are imported or contain a high proportion of imported goods.

Whether one is considering either the capital costs of equipment or the paperwork burden required to report on compliance, the compliance costs associated with regulations obviously require that funds be diverted from other sources (such as future investment or employee-associated costs) or that increased costs ultimately be passed along to consumers. These added costs mean that businesses have less capital available for either increasing the wages of current employees or hiring new workers. In addition, the compliance costs associated with some regulation (such as filling out government-required forms) add nothing to a company's bottom line or level of productivity.

Therefore, it is easy to see why the employment effects of regulation are of special interest to policymakers and to the public. A survey conducted in 1992 for the National Commission for Employment Policy—an independent executive branch agency that advised the President and Congress on employment and training issues until its demise on September 30, 1995—found that the regulatory review practices and models and methods used in key federal regulatory agencies to examine regulatory impacts did not explicitly or systematically take potential employment effects into consideration during the review process, in enforcement decisions, or in the setting of an overall framework for regulatory policy.

The commission also found that few good regulatory analyses addressed such effects as limiting the number of new employees hired, dismissing current employees, and lowering salaries or wages (where such flexibility exists). Even in those rare instances when employment effects were considered, they were taken into account only in terms of the general category of "employee," making no distinctions among skill levels, functions, or corporate roles. There were also questions about the validity of analyses that addressed the dislocation effects of particular regulations due to the closure of noncompliant facilities or the movement of facilities out of the country.

In addition to the problem of adequately addressing employment effects in individual regulatory actions, accounting for economywide employment effects due to regulatory change is very difficult. The government does not view or review regulations as part of broadly conceived, coherent programs to achieve particular goals. Individual regulatory decisions often reflect attempts to make specific rules to implement narrow congressional mandates. Many regulators typically focus only on the particular industry that they regulate; the overall, economywide impacts of the regulations on employment in other industries can be easily overlooked.

Even if a regulation does apply to one or a few sectors, the likely important employment effects that occur in other sectors due to the interconnections among sectors are largely ignored. Therefore, the use of economywide models to assess economywide employment effects is essential because so much regulatory activity applies to all sectors (i.e., health, safety, environment, affirmative action, and civil rights).

It is not surprising that throughout the regulatory process, government agencies are accused by industry of underestimating the jobs impact whereas regulatory agencies and public interest groups claim that industry estimates are usually way too high. To demonstrate how inadequately and imprecisely employment effects are addressed in the regulatory process, the U.S. Department of Labor estimated that the twenty-five regulations that it planned to promulgate during 1992 would have compliance costs ranging from $1 billion to more than $6 billion. The number of jobs lost was estimated to be between 21,000 and 124,000.

As another example, the luxury tax imposed during the Bush administration almost closed down the domestic boat-building industry, contrary to the original projections. Revenue estimates from that tax proved wrong, as boat purchasers either held off purchases or bought their boats from overseas suppliers. It was estimated that imposition of the luxury tax caused the layoff of approximately 100,000 workers nationwide, and that the federal government paid out $5 in unemployment compensation costs for every dollar collected on the tax.

It is the confusion over the types of issues raised here that makes it imperative for regulatory decisionmakers, legislators, and others with interests in regulatory policy to pay greater attention to the employment effects of regulation. This book should help to raise that awareness.

Chapter 2 provides a history of the regulatory process. Chapter 3 presents an overview of the existing literature on the economic and employment costs of regulation. Literature dealing with the general effects and attendant costs of regulation, and with the employment effects of regulation, are summarized.

Chapter 4 describes the major tools and techniques available to federal agencies to measure the employment effects of regulation. The chapter also reports on the results of interviews with selected federal agency officials charged with carrying out assessments of the effects of proposed regulations and enforcement decisions and with scholars and observers of the regulatory process.

Chapter 5 builds on the foundation laid out in Chapter 4 and discusses the evolution of the federal regulatory review and oversight process, and selected political, institutional, and judicial issues that have influenced that evolution.

Chapter 6 offers several approaches for improving government-wide management of the federal regulatory process. The centerpiece of the approaches recommended in this book are (1) a requirement that employment and wage effects be addressed explicitly in the regulatory decision-making process; (2) the use of state-of-the-art analytical tools to assess broad impacts of regulation on employment patterns and wage levels throughout the economy as well as the cumulative effects of regulatory programs (rather than only the more limited effects of specific rules); and (3) policy and institutional approaches that address deficiencies in the current regulatory decision-making process.

The book also contains four appendices. They include a discussion on the use of computable general equilibrium models to estimate the employment effects of regulation; Executive Order (EO) 12866 of September 30, 1993, on Regulatory Planning and Review; guidelines for the economic analysis of federal regulations issued under EO 12866; and a topical bibliography of studies on the effects of regulation.

Regulatory reform actions taken by the 104th Congress and even some of the recent reforms announced by the Clinton administration reflect dissatisfaction with the current regulatory regime. As part of its Contract with America, the House of Representatives has passed bills requiring extensive risk analysis for proposed regulations; the Senate is considering provisions for congressional oversight of proposed, significant regulations. Even the Clinton administration has proposed minimal changes to speed up the regulatory development procedures at the U.S. Environmental Protection Agency and the Food and Drug Administration.

Nevertheless, the impact of regulations on employment still receives scant attention. That is why this book is necessary. It addresses the extent to which potential employment effects are taken into consideration in the federal government's regulatory decision-making process and how that process can be improved by Congress and the president in the review of specific regulations and in overall regulatory planning governmentwide.

A Brief History of Federal Regulation of Business and Society

The legal basis of regulation is found in Article I, Section 8, of the Constitution, commonly called the "commerce clause," allowing Congress "to regulate commerce with foreign nations and among the several states." Over the past century, regulation has been justified on the basis of curbing natural monopolies (utilities), protecting public safety (defense and police functions), controlling profits (rent control), mitigating negative externalities (pollution, when it is not accounted for in the cost of producing a product), and informational deficiencies (drug safety regulation). This chapter describes the history of the federal government's involvement in the regulation of economic activity and identifies requirements for cost/benefit and similar analyses. It also pays particular attention to the regulation of employment and labor markets.

THE FIRST PHASE OF FEDERAL REGULATION, 1880–1929

The type of regulation implemented during the first phase of federal regulation may be classified as economic regulation. Economic regulation covered the prices of the goods or services provided in a particular industry, or the quantities sold, or other economic aspects of a specific industry or market, such as the number of firms in the industry or the freedom of firms to enter or leave the industry. Economic regulation is also known as vertical regulation, affecting the economic structures of entire industries such as utilities, railroads, and transportation.

This phase took place between the 1880s and the Great Depression of 1929. In these early years of regulatory activity, regulation provided some companies with a sense of market stability. Critics of early regulation viewed that stability as protection and a barrier to the entry of competitors to a particular market. In fact, the original goal of much of the regulation of this era was to protect or help companies in a competitive environment, such as trucking. Regulation took the forms of licensing, financial reporting procedures, copyright and patent protection, and antimonopoly restrictions.

In the latter half of the nineteenth century, rate discrimination and other abuses in the railroad industry came to public attention. Industry efforts at self-regulation and state regulation failed to stem those problems. In 1887, Congress addressed that problem by establishing the first federal regulatory agency, the Interstate Commerce Commission (ICC). As the ICC was largely an information-gathering agency, effective regulation of the railroads did not begin until the passage of the Hepburn Act of 1906. Additional legislation, such as the Mann-Elkins Act of 1906, extended the ICC's regulatory authority to include telephone, telegraph, and cable and wireless companies engaged in interstate commerce. Congress also extended the federal government's regulatory reach over antitrust through a variety of laws from 1890 to 1914, and regulation of banking and the currency supply in 1913, with the establishment of the Federal Reserve System. The first directive from Congress to a regulatory agency to address costs and benefits came in the Rivers and Harbors Act of 1902.

THE SECOND PHASE OF FEDERAL REGULATION, 1930–1960

In response to the Depression of 1929, the federal government broadened its regulatory powers. This second phase of federal regulatory activity was considered appropriate to curtail monopolistic practices, correct failures in the market, and control the prices and practices of public services such as utilities, transport, and banking.

The powers of existing regulatory agencies, such as the Federal Reserve Board and the Federal Trade Commission, were expanded to address alleged weaknesses in the economy. New, stronger rules were also developed for agricultural price supports, union formation, and manmade monopolies (such as oil). New rules and new agencies were created for various sectors or industries throughout the 1930s:

- banking regulation and deposit insurance against loss and the Federal Deposit Insurance Corporation (1933);
- securities regulation and the Securities and Exchange Commission (1934);
- communications regulation and the Federal Communications Commission (1934);
- airline regulation and the Civil Aeronautics Board (1938).

This period was also critical for developing the framework for employment and labor market regulations. The Davis-Bacon Public Construction Act, passed in 1931, required private contractors working on federally funded construction projects to pay wages at least equal to prevailing wages in the region. The National Labor Relations Board Act (1935) required the government to monitor union elections and rules on unfair labor practices; the Social Security Act directed every state to adopt an unemployment insurance law that imposed a compulsory payroll tax on all employees. Finally, the Fair Labor Standards Act (1938) established the first nationwide minimum wage law.

Following World War II, the wartime controls were lifted and government regulatory activity focused mostly on enforcing the laws passed during the New Deal era of the 1930s. The major regulatory actions during this period addressed economic growth in general (through the Employment Act of 1946); mergers (through the Celler-Kefauver Act of 1951); and energy (through a combination of Federal Power Commission rules on natural gas pricing and mandates from President Eisenhower on oil import quotas).

During the first two phases, it was believed that the solutions to such problems as environmental pollution and health and safety protection were the responsibility of the industry affected. As American society began to regard this as increasingly insufficient over time, individual states began enacting laws and regulations to reduce the environmental, health, and safety risks to the public. Nevertheless, those early interventions were limited in scope and authority; the first requirement for a formal cost/benefit analysis procedure did not appear until the Flood Control Act of 1936.

THE THIRD PHASE OF FEDERAL REGULATION, 1961–Present

In response to increased public pressure and a professed need to protect the public interest, the Congress devoted a great deal of effort in the 1960s and 1970s to passing new laws and establishing new agencies to protect the environment, promote workplace safety, and improve consumer products. This third phase of federal regulatory activity resulted in a dramatic increase in the level and scope of government regulation of business and the economy. Called "social regulation," regulatory action was directed toward social, rather than economic, goals (although we all recognize that there were and are significant economic ramifications to pursuing social goals via regulation). More parties both inside and outside government became interested in and affected by regulation and the regulatory process. Social regulation applied to all goods and services in all industries in all sectors of the U.S. economy. Through its focus on matters common to many firms, such as pollution control, social regulation affected prices and quantities indirectly, by specifying product or production characteristics.

Most economic regulation is implemented by agencies that are statutorily independent of the executive branch and were established during the first two phases of U.S. regulatory history. In contrast, most social regulation is conducted by agencies within the executive branch that either were created during the 1970s or saw their mandates broadened significantly during that decade. The regulatory areas and agencies established during this period included environmental protection and the Environmental Protection Agency (1970); highway safety and the National Highway Traffic Safety Administration (1966); and product safety and the Consumer Product Safety Commission (1972). Employment and labor market-related regulatory areas and agencies established during this period included civil rights and the Equal Employment Opportunity Commission (1972); workplace safety and the Occupational Safety and Health Administration (1970); and mine safety and the Mine Safety and Health Administration (1977).

Of course, economic regulation did not vanish from the scene. The early part of the decade saw an almost unprecedented regulatory act by the federal government: in August 1971, President Richard Nixon imposed wage and price controls on most of the U.S. economy (excepting some sectors, such as agriculture). Although that action was taken as a way of stemming inflation, many critics believed that the controls only delayed the onset of higher inflation, rather than wringing it out of the economy.

With the exception of controls on crude oil and petroleum products, the program was phased out during 1973 and 1974. Critics also believed that the phasing out of controls in some sectors but not others also caused serious disruptions in the economy. With respect to energy, the Nixon program and the partial decontrol that followed it decreased the incentives for exploring new energy sources and for building new refineries.

As the reach of the federal regulatory agencies expanded, two other phenomena occurred. First, there was strong pressure building to deregulate those markets where government intervention had restricted competition without increasing the benefits to the general public or to consumers. Deregulation gained as a valid approach of government management as the market was recognized increasingly as a superior mechanism (to the government) for allocating resources. In addition, many special interest groups took the position that economic regulation of specific industries had not always succeeded in ensuring the most efficient use of resources and the most economical range of services for consumers. Many aspects of economic regulation of specific industries had been rendered obsolete by new technologies. Therefore, the latter part of the 1970s saw the deregulation of major service industries, including airlines, trucking, telecommunications, and banking and financial services.

Second, White House oversight over the regulatory agencies and proposed rules increased through a more aggressive use of regulatory review and analytical tools such as cost/benefit analysis. As noted, federal regulation was primarily economic and largely industry-specific prior to 1970. There was little need for a formal regulatory review process. Most regulatory reviews took place either informally before a regulation was promulgated or by challenges in the courts after it was promulgated. The rationale for increased cost/benefit analysis was that such a tool would lead to a more efficient allocation of resources by subjecting the public sector to some level of quantitative restraints.

The formal framework for regulatory development and enforcement has become a topic of public debate and a point of contention between legislative and executive units (see Chapter 5). Some of the issues raised were addressed through legislation, such as the "Government in the Sunshine Act of 1976" (P.L.

94–409), whose objective was to make all governmental activities more "transparent" to the general public through open meetings.

By 1980, the impact of regulation was becoming so pervasive throughout the American economy, and its effects were becoming so burdensome, particularly for small and medium–sized businesses as well as local governments, that two major pieces of legislation were passed to mitigate these effects. The Paperwork Reduction Act of 1980 (P.L. 96–511) and the Regulatory Flexibility Act of 1980 (P.L. 96–354) dealt, respectively, with attempts to limit the paperwork required in complying with government regulations and other programs, and with consideration of the differential impact of social, health, safety, and environmental regulation on smaller private (as well as public) entities.

CONCLUSION

The economywide impacts of regulation on employment were rarely a factor in regulatory decision making during the three phases of regulation. Rules were generally adopted, or industries were deregulated, on more political, social, or economywide grounds. As will be shown in the next chapter, the employment implications of regulation were a consideration only for employment-specific rules, such as wage and hour regulations, workplace composition, and union practices.

The Economic and Employment Effects of Regulation

The first part of this chapter summarizes the existing literature on the ways in which government regulations affect the U.S. economy. The results of five major studies are presented, as well as the findings of other studies that examine specific aspects of regulation and the economy. The second part of this chapter describes how current studies address the employment effects of specific labor market regulations. Specific types of regulation are discussed, including regulations that directly and indirectly affect employment levels and wages. The final section of this chapter addresses measurement of the effects of taxation on economic growth and employment and draws important parallels between the effects of taxation and regulation.

THE ECONOMYWIDE IMPACTS OF REGULATION

Analysts have spent a deal of time, energy, and money in trying to determine the direct impact that regulations have on specific industries and the economy as a whole. The results of these analyses are, at best, controversial. Rarely do the opposite sides of a debate agree. Organized labor and public interest groups are accused of downplaying the costs of compliance. Businesses are criticized for supposedly inflating compliance costs.

Before discussing the specific results of these studies, it is useful to describe the different ways in which regulatory costs may be calculated and impacts may be felt. It is generally agreed that the effects of regulation on business and the economy can be divided into three broad categories: direct, indirect, and induced (Weidenbaum 1980).

Direct costs are the costs of compliance with regulations. These costs are likely to be borne directly by corporations in the near term, but passed on to workers and consumers through lower wages and higher prices in the longer term.

The higher prices reduce the demand for the product by the consumer, and that has a direct and negative effect on employment levels (i.e., a first-order effect). It is usually this cost that is examined in most regulatory analyses.

Indirect costs of regulation are associated with the actions necessary to change a company's way of doing business in order to comply with federal government mandates. Those costs could include the growing paperwork imposed on business, time delays due to the regulatory process, and losses of productivity, all of which can have adverse effects on employment. Firms also respond to the direct and indirect effects of regulation by cutting back on new capital investment as funds are diverted to meet government-mandated requirements.

Finally, the induced costs of regulation include those activities that are not undertaken because of regulatory constraints and burdens. These costs affect the pace of technological innovation and development, the ability to finance growth, and the capability to perform basic functions of producing goods and services. Regulation thus places a "drag" on the nation's overall economic growth that can have a negative impact on investment, innovation, and global competitiveness. As a result of the induced costs of regulation, scientific progress is slowed and the economy/society experiences a reduced rate of introduction of new products and improved production processes.

It is important to recognize that there will always be adjustment costs in terms of labor relocations and possible unemployment from any change in regulation, whether it is the imposition of new regulations or elimination of existing regulations. Yet, regulation per se does not have to lead to permanently higher unemployment levels. In the absence of labor market rigidities and distortions that inhibit the wage level from adjusting to changing market conditions, unemployment would simply be a result of friction in the job search process. To some extent, therefore, changes in unemployment will be caused by changes in regulations and not the mere existence of such regulations. The same cannot be concluded with respect to wage rates. With fully flexible labor markets, the mere existence of regulatory policies is likely to cause a permanent drop in real wages.

Weidenbaum (1980) summarizes two additional ways in which the direct, indirect, and induced costs of regulation may be felt: to taxpayers for supporting budgetary expenditures of federal regulatory agencies; and to the industrial and commercial base from the loss of small businesses that cannot meet the burden of regulation.

Although regulation imposes tremendous costs, economic benefits to society are expected to accrue from it. However, these benefits may accrue to individuals and groups in the near term but only to the larger society over the longer term. Some regulations may have very high compliance costs with negligible, negative, or unmeasurable benefits. In addition, although there may be very significant net benefits to society from a costly regulation, it may be that an alternative (or market-based) approach to a proposed regulation could produce the same benefit at a lower cost and with less disruption to economic processes.

The literature on regulation broadly falls into three categories. The first category, and by far the largest, consists of numerous studies that focus on an individual regulation, or a particular kind of regulation, in isolation. The second category addresses those studies that attempt to measure the economic effects of deregulating selected industries. The third category consists of a small number of studies that present broad overviews of regulation, dealing with many types of regulation together rather than one particular type in isolation. Each of these latter studies is largely a synthesis of other studies, combining cost estimates for particular kinds of regulation to arrive at a figure for the cost of regulation in toto.[1] Studies comprising those categories are listed in the Topical Bibliography in Appendix D.

Studies Dealing with Individual Regulations in Isolation

The vast majority of the studies in the category of studies of individual regulations focus on the total cost of the regulation(s) to society, measured in dollars. Specific kinds of costs or effects—such as reduced employment levels, foreign investment, or international competitiveness—are not normally delineated. In most instances, only one or two specific kinds of costs may actually have been counted, such as the cost to the government of administering and enforcing the regulations or direct private sector expenditures on compliance. Larger considerations, such as reductions in consumer welfare or declines in innovation, are rarely addressed.

However, some studies have focused on the particular effects that are especially relevant to the kind of regulation being examined—usually in the area of social regulation. For example, several studies have examined the effects of federal drug regulation on the availability and price of potential life saving drugs, focusing mainly on the number of new medicines introduced each year.[2] Studies have also been performed to examine the effect of federal minimum fuel economy standards on the number of deaths and serious injuries that will occur over the lifetime of each model year's automobiles and trucks (see Crandall and Graham, 1989).

Studies Looking at Deregulation

Like most other studies within the literature on regulation, these studies on the effects of deregulation (either before or after the fact) focus on the total cost of the regulation(s) to society, measured in dollars. However, because their focus is on deregulation, they are usually cast in terms of the benefits to be obtained from deregulation rather than the costs imposed by regulation.

The studies dealing with deregulation illustrate two important points: (1) the difficulty of ascertaining *all* of the costs of any regulation and (2) the fact that, as a result of this difficulty, the true costs of a regulation can often be significantly greater than what might be thought. This can be seen, for example, by looking at studies dealing with the regulation of transportation. A comparison of such studies shows that estimates of the costs of transportation regulation made before the partial deregulation that occurred in the late 1970s and early 1980s were consistently and substantially below the estimated levels of benefits that were cited in the aftermath of deregulation.

For example, ex ante estimates of the costs of trucking regulation ranged from $1.5 billion to $8.2 billion (Moore 1978), while an ex post study (Owen 1988, based on Delaney 1986) estimated the cost reductions due to trucking deregulation to be on the order of $40.5 to $65.5 billion. Ex ante estimates of the costs of airline regulation ranged from $0.7 billion to $2.9 billion (Hahn and Hird 1991, based on Litan and Nordhaus 1983), whereas ex post estimates of the benefits of deregulation ranged from $4.8 billion (Caves et al. 1987) to $15.6 billion (Morrison and Winston 1986). An ex ante estimate of the costs of railroad regulation (Winston 1985) put the figure at $6.8 billion. Although one ex post study of deregulation (Boyer 1987) found cost savings of only $102 *million*, another (Barnekov and Kleit 1988) suggested that the model used in the first study was misspecified, and that the actual efficiency gains (estimated by using the same data but, in their view, a better-specified model) were between $9.7 and $16.9 *billion* annually.[3]

In each case, the discrepancy appeared to result in whole or in part from some unanticipated change in technology—either a change in the technology of providing a service (e.g., the hub-and-spoke routing system used by airlines) or a change in the technology of using a service (e.g., "just-in-time" inventory management, used by companies that ship products by rail or truck). In each case, the change in technology either was made possible or at least was partly abetted or facilitated by deregulation. Our inability to anticipate *all* of the technological innovations that might be possible in the absence of regulation constitutes one important reason why the true total costs of regulation are inherently difficult to know and inherently likely to be underestimated.

Studies Dealing with Regulation as a Whole

To date there have been only five principal studies that have attempted to estimate the total cost of all regulations taken together. Each has attempted to build on the works that came before it by incorporating more recent data, and by including cost estimates for categories of regulation that were omitted from the previous studies.

The first comprehensive study attempting to estimate the costs of regulation in toto was performed by Weidenbaum and DeFina (1978). They present an estimate of the annual cost of regulation, measured in dollars per year, as $66 billion in 1976, or $115 billion in 1991 dollars. The second study, by Litan and Nordhaus (1983), using a similar methodology to estimate the cost of regulation, offers a cost ranging from \$35 to \$91 billion in 1977, or approximately \$77 billion to \$200 billion per year in 1991 dollars.

The third major study of this type was prepared by Hahn and Hird (1991). Using 1988 data, they make several improvements on the previous studies. The most significant improvements were the following:

- attempting to include benefits as well as costs in their analysis;
- distinguishing between efficiency costs ("real economic losses that one group suffers, yet another group cannot reclaim as benefits") and transfers ("a redistribution of benefits from one group to another that has no impact on total economic output");
- incorporating estimates for several kinds of regulation (most notably trade restrictions) that had been omitted from previous estimates of the total cost of regulation.

Hahn and Hird estimate the total cost of economic and social regulation to be between \$142 billion and \$177 billion per year as of 1988, in 1991 dollars. If transfers are included, then their figure for total cost would be between \$340 billion and \$418 billion per year, in 1991 dollars. On the other hand, they estimate the benefits of social regulation to be between \$48 billion and \$209 billion per year as of 1988, in 1991 dollars. They find no benefits—other than transfers—due to economic regulation. If transfers are counted as benefits—as they must be if they are also counted as costs—then Hahn and Hird's figure for total benefits would be between \$246 billion and \$450 billion per year, in 1991 dollars. Either way, their figure for the net benefit or cost of all regulation in toto comes out to somewhere between a net cost of about \$94 billion per year and a net benefit of about \$32 billion per year, in 1991 dollars.

The Hahn and Hird study included an excellent and comprehensive survey of relevant previous work. Subsequent studies have used the Hahn and Hird study as a starting point.

The fourth major study of the total cost of all regulations was by Hopkins (1991).[4] Hopkins used the Hahn and Hird study as a starting point but went beyond it in two important respects. Hopkins presented a series of estimates for the years 1977 through 2000, in order to give a picture of how the cost of regulation has changed or will change, if present trends continue, over time. He also included another major category of regulation that had not been included in previous estimates—"process regulation," which consists mainly of the administrative cost to businesses of complying with government-imposed record-keeping and paperwork requirements and to state and local governments of responding to federal mandates.

Hopkins did not attempt to incorporate benefits (like Hahn and Hird); he included transfers as costs but set them out separately, giving the figures both with and without transfers. He estimated the total annual cost of federal regulation as of 1992, including transfer costs of economic regulation, to be between \$413 billion and \$533 billion in 1988 dollars, or between \$475 billion and \$614 billion per year in 1991 dollars. However, this figure is artificially low because Hopkins deliberately understated the transfer costs of economic regulation.

Hopkins derived his figures for the transfer costs of economic regulation from Hahn and Hird (1991), who reported a lower bound of $172.1 billion and an upper bound of $209.5 billion, in 1988 dollars. However, Hopkins averaged Hahn and Hird's lower and upper bounds to get a new estimate of $191 billion, which he then treated as an upper bound and arbitrarily divided by 2 to get a new lower bound of $95 billion. If Hopkins had used Hahn and Hird's original lower and upper bounds, his figure for the gross cost of all federal regulations as of 1992 would have been between $564 billion and $635 billion per year, in 1991 dollars.

Hopkins also revised his estimate of the total cost of complying with federal paperwork requirements. The figure he reported—$100 billion per year as of 1992, measured in 1988 dollars—was based on the federal government's Information Collection Budget for Fiscal Year 1990. His new figure for 1992—based on the Information Collection Budget for Fiscal Year 1991—was $127.38 billion per year in 1988 dollars.[5] If the new figure is substituted for the old figure, the resulting figure for the total direct cost of all federal regulations, including transfer costs of economic regulation, is between $595 billion and $667 billion per year, measured in 1991 dollars.

The fifth, and most recent, study dealing with the costs of regulation in toto is Bord and Laffer (1992). Their study includes estimates for several kinds of regulation that were not included in previous studies, including regulation of electric utilities, some kinds of banking regulation,[6] and state tort law. They also include estimates for the Clean Air Act Amendments of 1990 and the Americans with Disabilities Act of 1990, both of which were enacted after Hahn and Hird and Hopkins did their research. Also attempting to take account of these indirect effects (which are more difficult to measure), Bord and Laffer estimated the total burden of state and federal regulation to be between $1 billion and $2 trillion per year, ignoring benefits, and between $810 billion and $1.7 trillion per year even after subtracting benefits.[7]

Despite the progress that has been made to date in terms of adding estimates for categories of regulation that had previously been omitted, none of these studies comes close to having a complete accounting of regulatory costs. Even the three most recent and comprehensive of these studies still omit a number of major categories of federal regulation, including important aspects of the regulation of banking and financial services; civil rights and antitrust laws; the federal minimum wage; and other recently enacted federal legislation that is regulatory in nature. Moreover, only the Bord and Laffer study (1992) even attempts to include any kinds of state regulation, and it still omits many other important kinds of state and local regulation.

None of the five studies focused on regulation in toto in general deals in a satisfactory way with the effects of regulation on the levels of wages and labor employment. The study by Bord and Laffer explicitly notes the existence and importance of these effects[8] but makes no attempt to quantify them.

Static versus Dynamic Effects

Even within the categories of regulation that *are* considered in the literature, only two or three kinds of costs are normally counted: the cost to the government of administering and enforcing the regulations, direct private sector expenditures on compliance, and reductions in consumer welfare. All of these costs are static in the sense that they do not include any kind of productivity effects.

Productivity growth is the increase over time in output for a given level of inputs (labor and capital). In general, regulations adversely affect productivity by increasing costs and reducing output for a given level of inputs. Studies have consistently found that high-regulation industries achieve lower productivity growth than low-regulation industries.

Specifically, regulation can affect productivity, growth, and output in a variety of ways:

- by reducing the returns to entrepreneurship by structuring markets and transactions to preclude innovation and the development of new technologies, manufacturing processes, and products;
- by reducing the amount of labor and capital that are employed in the regulated sectors of the economy, and in any nonregulated sectors as well to the extent that they depend on the outputs of the regulated sectors;
- by reducing savings, investment, and capital formation within the domestic economy;
- by reducing foreign investment;
- by causing firms to use different and less efficient combinations of labor and capital in the production process.

Although the existence and importance of regulation's various effects on productivity, growth, and output are often acknowledged in the literature on regulation, few studies have attempted to quantify these effects. Moreover, those studies dealt with only one or two kinds of regulation (principally environmental and workplace safety regulation);[9] the productivity effects of most regulations, and of regulation in toto, remain quantitatively unexamined.

Furthermore, none of these studies considered the effects of regulation on innovation and technology growth, even though in the long run these may be the most significant effects of all. Effects on innovation and technology are often noted and discussed qualitatively but are virtually impossible to quantify. A few economists (see, e.g., Romer 1990) have begun to attempt to model technology growth. King and Rebello (1993) posit that with "endogenous growth" models in which technology growth responds to policy, taxes, or implied taxes (such as regulation), regulation affects long-run growth rates and thus could have very large effects on welfare. However, so far no one has attempted to apply models of sustained endogenous productivity growth to regulation.

Effects on Productivity and Output

Nearly all of the studies that have attempted to quantify the indirect effects of regulation on productivity and output have found these effects to be substantial[10]—so large, in fact, as to suggest that these indirect effects may be as large as, and perhaps even significantly larger than, the direct effects that are more frequently measured. For example, Jorgenson and Wilcoxen (1989, 1990) and Hazilla and Kopp (1990)—two general studies of the effects of environmental regulation on economic growth that employ sophisticated economic models of society—both show that reductions in labor supply, savings and investment, growth in the capital stock, and output tend to accumulate over time. As a result, the total costs imposed by environmental regulation end up being more than twice as large in Jorgenson and Wilcoxen (1990) and over three times as large in the case of Hazilla and Kopp (1990) as the direct compliance costs alone. These studies suggest that the true cost of regulation may be significantly larger than conventional estimates.

Only Bord and Laffer (1992) (of the five principal studies) attempts to take account of the indirect effects of regulation on productivity and output. In an *ad hoc* way, they extrapolate indirect costs from the direct costs. The other four studies confine themselves to direct compliance and enforcement expenditures and static consumer welfare costs. Because these four studies omit indirect effects on productivity and output, they may substantially underestimate the total cost of regulation.

Interactions between Regulations

The five principal studies simply take cost estimates for individual regulations and then add them together to arrive at a figure for the cost of regulation *in toto*. This constitutes a second reason why these studies may substantially underestimate the total cost of regulation, for the approach they use overlooks the importance of interdependence effects.

A regulation cannot be fully evaluated in isolation. The existence of other regulations can make a given regulation more costly than it would have been in the absence of the other rules. Likewise, the imposition of additional regulations can make previously existing regulations more costly than they were before. Consequently, the true cost of any new regulation is not the cost that it would impose in isolation, but the addition that it would make to the burden caused by all regulations taken together. In terms of the burden regulation places on the economy, the whole can be greater than the sum of the parts.

The same point applies to the benefits of regulation. Insofar as regulations produce benefits as well as costs, there may be situations in which regulations complement each other, so that changing or eliminating one without making a compensating adjustment in the other can disrupt the balance and increase the total cost of regulation. Sometimes a regulation that imposes costs on one sector of the economy can increase the productivity of other sectors. For example, many businesses and manufacturing processes (e.g., agricultural production and food and beverage processing) depend on clean air or water. Properly designed environmental protection regulation can reduce costs for others (e.g., by eliminating the need to undertake expensive water purification measures) and enhance performance, output, and employment in these industries. Here as well, interdependence effects can be important.

THE EMPLOYMENT EFFECTS OF LABOR MARKET RULES

Relatively little attention has been paid to the overall effect of regulation on employment levels. Studies examining the effects of specific regulations or types of regulation (e.g., pollution control) occasionally consider employment effects but almost never do so in a rigorous and systematic fashion. Similarly, the literature on labor economics by and large has not addressed regulation as a factor affecting employment levels, except in regard to those regulations that are directly related to labor markets and employment.

A small portion of the extensive body of literature dealing with the general determinants of wage and employment levels deals with certain kinds of regulation—those that are directly related to labor markets and employment, covering such corporate activities as hiring and firing, compensation, promotion, union relations, and pension plans. They affect almost all companies that have more than one employee, in all sectors of the economy. These broadly applied regulations fall largely under the jurisdiction of the U.S. Department of Labor (and its many bureaus and administrations) and the Equal Employment Opportunity Commission. A somewhat narrower range of labor market regulation is administered by, inter alia, the National Labor Relations Board and the Pension Benefit Guarantee Corporation.

Two principal kinds of effects are generally attributed to labor market regulations: effects on wage rates or total compensation levels, and effects on employment levels. Most of these regulations produce a mixture of both kinds of effects, although the balance can vary, depending on the regulation in question and the particular circumstances.

Certain regulations (which are referred to here as labor market rules) have clear and direct impacts on the cost of hiring and employing workers, thereby acting as a tax on job creation and employment. These include wage and hour regulations (i.e. minimum wage, Davis-Bacon on construction), labor relations requirements on business (i.e., federal labor laws regulating employers' dealings with their employees and with labor unions), specific areas of government involvement (i.e., safety, compensation, retirement, and mandated benefits such as child care), workplace composition and hiring and firing processes (i.e., Civil Rights Act of 1964, affirmative action, and EEO rules), and union versus nonunion status. It has been claimed that these rules limit the employment opportunities of youth, women, racial minorities, and the not-yet-skilled; reduce the viability of smaller firms; add upward pressure on all wages; and increase marginally the general price level (Heldman et al. 1981).

The only attempt to quantify the impact of those labor market rules on the economy was found in Heldman et al. (1981). That analysis, fifteen years ago, estimated that the gross benefits to be realized from eliminating many of the labor market rules (including the Fair Labor Standards Act; Davis-Bacon; Unemployment Insurance; the federal budget portion of the Comprehensive Employment and Training Act; and the administrative cost savings of the EEO, OSHA, and the National Labor Relations Act) were slightly more than $170 billion (in 1979 dollars).

Several areas in which government has regulated labor markets and employment are described in the discussion that follows.

Compensation and Hours of Work

Among the oldest regulations that affect labor markets are those related to compensation and hours of work. The first category of rules in this area includes those that affect compensation by setting basic rates of pay. These rules are developed under the Fair Labor Standards Act of 1938, which sets the federal minimum wage law; regulates the length of the standard work week and rates of pay for overtime work; and restricts the use of child labor. The Public Construction Act (Davis-Bacon), Public Contracts Act (Walsh-Healy), and Service Contracts Act (O'Hara-McNamara) set pay, hours, and working conditions for, respectively, construction, supply contracts, and service contracts. The second category of rules addresses equal pay. These include the Equal Pay Act and the Vocational Rehabilitation Act.

Minimum wage rules are the clearest example of a labor market regulation that reduces employment levels. A large body of literature posits that minimum wage laws reduce the employment of workers with low skill levels, whose time is simply not worth what the government would require an employer to pay for it. This especially affects younger, less experienced workers, and workers who have had less education. The focus of the disagreement in the literature at present is on the size and significance of the employment reductions caused by the minimum wage requirement. In 1981, the Minimum Wage Study Commission reported that increases in the minimum wage negatively affected employment by decreasing employment below the level that would otherwise have occurred in the absence of a minimum wage increase. The commission found that a 10 percent increase in the minimum wage caused a 1 to 3 percent decrease in teenage employment.

Many studies note that although the minimum wage law reduces employment of low-skilled workers, it may increase employment of medium-skilled workers, who, to some extent, can be used in lieu of the low-skilled workers whose labor the minimum wage renders too expensive. Workers whose wages are somewhat above the legal minimum, but not too much above it, fall into this category. The fact that such workers often are unionized is widely thought to account for the fact that labor unions have traditionally supported the minimum wage law, even though most union members earn wages above the legal minimum.

However, even given this view, any increase in employment of medium-skilled workers will necessarily be smaller than the decrease in employment of low-skilled workers. Moreover, in the long run, even employment of medium-skilled and high-skilled workers can be reduced by the minimum wage. (For present purposes, high-skilled workers can be thought of as any workers whose wages and skill levels are so high that they cannot practically or profitably be substituted for low-skilled workers.) The reason is that medium-skilled and high-skilled workers need low-skilled workers with whom to work. If fewer low-skilled workers are employed as a resukt of the minimum wage, the productivity of other workers will be reduced, or will grow more slowly over time.[11]

In the case of medium-skilled workers, it might be some time before the reduction, if any, in wages and/or employment due to reduced productivity could offset the increase in wages and/or employment due to the increased demand by firms to use medium-skilled labor as a substitute for low-skilled labor. However, in the case of high-skilled workers for whom the substitution effects of an increase in the minimum wage are negligible, the negative employment effects, if any, could start to set in immediately. In each case, the negative employment effects would be in the form of slower growth in wages or employment rather than an outright reduction in wage or employment levels. Consequently, the negative employment effects will be difficult to detect in the short term.

Supporting the findings of the Minimum Wage Study Commission, a February 1993 report on the minimum wage released by the Employment Policies Institute (EPI) concluded that employment is reduced by 1 to 2 percent for every 10 percent increase in the minimum wage (Neumark 1993). The reduction in employment means fewer opportunities for teens and young adults and for on-the-job training opportunities, and an increased burden on the unemployment compensation system. The report acknowledged that increases in the minimum wage raised the wages of already-employed, low-wage workers, but such increases were offset by a reduction in the number of workers who were employed. The report also showed that increases in the minimum wage have lagged effects: that is, the wage increase does not have its full effect on employment levels for more than a year.

Another study released by EPI in 1993 (Taylor 1993) examined the impact of wage increases in the retail sector in California. This second study supported the proposal that an increase in the minimum wage decreased overall employment, but went one step further by reporting that the wage increases had their most pronounced and negative effects impacts in California's least affluent counties (ETR 1993, Passell 1993).

A small number of economists (David Card, Lawrence Katz, and Alan Krueger) have reported on new studies that they claim demonstrate that the minimum wage has no effect on employment levels and wages. Those studies were used by the Clinton administration to defend or justify its calls for an increase in the minimum wage. However, those studies have been somewhat refuted because of problems in their methodology and offset by new studies on the impact of the minimum wage on teenage employment (by Bruce Fallick) and on poverty rates (by John Addison and McKinley Blackburn) that found generally negative impacts associated with increases in the minimum wage.

Wage-setting laws, such as the Davis-Bacon Act, also affect employment levels and wages. Although the intent of these rules is to secure a particular wage level by mandating that workers at federally funded projects be paid at a level equal to the local prevailing wage, they discriminate against small businesses that otherwise could not afford to pay the high wage level and therefore prevent the employment of more workers and serve as a barrier to market entry. In addition, the research supports the proposition that the rules increase the construction costs of federally supported projects by .01 percent to 11 percent. In addition to the direct payroll costs, these rules mandate extensive paperwork and reporting requirements that add to the cost of compliance. That extra burden also falls more heavily on small firms.

Mandated Benefits

A variety of laws have been enacted and regulations promulgated requiring employers to provide various benefits or alternative forms of compensation to their employees such as health insurance, unemployment insurance, workers' compensation, retirement benefits (under the Employee Retirement Income Security Act), and child care. A recent example of mandated benefits is the Family and Medical Leave Act of 1993. Mandated benefits may appear attractive from a public sector perspective because they confer advantages without a direct or immediate impact on public expenditure or revenue, but the cost is present nonetheless. Mandated benefits are, in effect, payroll taxes paid by everyone, most especially, those who become unemployed as a result of the increase in benefit costs.

Increased employee benefit costs (particularly mandated benefit costs) lead to negative trade-offs in terms of reduced employment, lower wages and salaries, and/or less money for other benefits, as employers seek to offset their increased costs of employing workers. By mandating levels of pay and overall compensation and removing such decisions from the business owner, the government may be discouraging a business from hiring new employees, encouraging the substitution of labor-intensive production techniques with those that are less labor-intensive, or prompting the relocation of a work site to a less regulated area.

If mandated benefit costs are not offset by lower wages and salaries or reduced expenditures on other benefits, then labor costs will rise and employment will be lower than it otherwise would have been. However, in the long run, such regulations will tend to have less of an impact on employment levels and will instead tend to reduce explicit wage and salary payments.

By mandating the provision of various benefits, the government merely alters the composition of compensation; it does not alter the total amount of compensation.[12] Therefore, if the total value of the employee's services remains unchanged, a government-mandated increase in benefits will ultimately lead to a reduction in the growth of wages over time. Although there may be some increase in employment costs and some reduction in employment levels over time, the ultimate reduction in wage levels may tend to moderate the long-run reduction in employment levels.

Another important impact of mandated benefits is the distributional effect. Clearly those workers who remain employed and qualify for the benefit gain insofar as their wages do not fall to offset benefit costs. Those workers who lose their jobs or are not hired because of increased labor costs are the big losers. Analyses suggest that the workers most likely to lose jobs as a result of higher mandated benefit costs are workers at or near minimum wage levels. This because their wages and payroll taxes cannot be reduced to offset higher costs for new benefits, and therefore the only way for employers to cut labor costs is to reduce employment. For example, the provision of employer financed mandatory health insurance for low-income workers is likely to have a particularly sharp effect on employment and on income distribution. These employment and distributional effects should be explicitly considered in comparing alternative health care reforms and other proposals that will raise employee benefit costs to employers.

A study by O'Neill and O'Neill (1993) estimated that the employment cost of the Clinton administration's 1994 proposed health care employer mandates legislation ranged from 790,000 jobs to 3.1 million jobs, depending on the administration's success in holding down health care costs. The study found that business would cover the cost of providing new health care benefits by reducing the number of employees or reducing salary levels. In fact, even the administration's own projections estimated that enactment of its health care program would result in a loss of 600 thousand jobs.

Industrial Relations

Many regulations govern relations among employers, labor unions, and employees (who might wish to join a labor union or to avoid being forced to join a labor union). These rules are developed under the Norris-LaGuardia Act; the National Labor Relations Act, also known as the Wagner Act; the Labor-Management Relations Act, better known as the Taft-Hartley Act; and the Labor-Management Reporting and Disclosure Act, better known as the Landrum-Griffin Act. The net effects of unions—and hence of federal regulations favoring unions—on employment levels, productivity, and wages have been debated extensively, but the results are inconclusive.

Employment Discrimination

Another type of employment-related regulation whose employment effects have not been conclusively established is employment discrimination legislation. Employment discrimination is addressed through regulations developed under a variety of laws, including Title VII of the Civil Rights Act of 1964, which prohibits discrimination in employment on the basis of race, color, religion, sex, or national origin; the Age Discrimination in Employment Act of 1967, which prohibits discrimination in employment on the basis of age and outlaws mandatory retirement provisions; and the new Americans with Disabilities Act, which prohibits discrimination in employment on the basis of physical or other disability.

Title VII has drawn the most attention in the literature. The most popular theory behind this regulatory approach is that civil rights laws do not affect total employment levels but increase job opportunities for minorities by opening up particular jobs that might otherwise have been foreclosed. Studies of employment discrimination rules have focused on changes in wages and in employment levels for blacks.

Various studies have documented increases in wage levels for blacks relative to whites following enactment of these employment provisions of the Civil Rights Act of 1964. Although many analysts agree that the wages for blacks probably grew faster as a result of antidiscrimination legislation, there is lingering disagreement over whether those wages are higher today than they otherwise would have been. Some argue that those wages would eventually have risen even without such legislation.

Similarly, various studies have documented increases in *relative* employment levels for blacks, but none of these studies has established whether *absolute* employment levels for blacks are higher or lower than they would have been in the absence of civil rights laws.[13] Studies focusing on relative employment levels assess the percentage of jobs within a given industry or economy occupied by blacks and whites, whereas a study focusing on absolute employment levels would consider the total number of jobs obtained by blacks and whites. If a policy increases the percentage of jobs held by blacks but reduces the total number of jobs, or causes the total number of jobs to grow more slowly than it otherwise would have, it may be possible for black employment to have increased relative to white employment but not absolutely.

Several legal scholars have argued that the enforcement and compliance costs act as a tax on employment: with each additional job an employer creates, his record-keeping burdens and chances of being sued increase. They assert that, at least as interpreted by the Supreme Court and amended by Congress, Title VII reduces *overall* employment levels but may either (1) increase job opportunities for minorities on balance, because the number of particular jobs that are opened to minorities exceeds the number of jobs that are lost to everyone, or (2) reduce employment levels *for minorities* on balance, because the reduction in overall employment levels is so large that it fully offsets the opening up to minorities of particular jobs that would otherwise have been foreclosed.[14] However, the proponents of such views have not yet established them empirically.

Equal employment and affirmative action rules became a point of controversy in 1995, as many members of Congress called for repeal or moderation of the existing regulatory system. It is expected that those laws and rules, and their application, will be important issues in elections for some time to come.

Occupational Safety and Health

Most regulations directed at promoting workplace safety and health are developed under the authority of the Occupational Safety and Health Act and the Mine Safety and Health Act. In analyzing the effects of these types of regulations on employment, it is generally maintained that workers whose working conditions are unpleasant or whose jobs entail an unusual degree of risk will normally be compensated for the unpleasant conditions or the extra risk through higher wages. Employers have to offer higher wages for risky or unpleasant jobs in order to attract enough workers to fill the jobs. However, if employers are forced to make their workplaces safer, they will no longer have to pay premium wages in order to attract workers. Most affected would be workers who prefer to endure the health or safety risks of coal mining, deep-sea diving, or coke-oven cleaning in return for higher wages. Employment levels, however, may be largely unaffected.[15]

Of course, for the kinds of occupations in question, it will normally cost an employer more to improve working conditions than it would cost to continue paying higher wages. If this were not the case, the employer would have chosen to improve the working conditions in order to avoid having to pay the higher wages in the first place. Consequently, forcing the employer to improve working conditions will necessarily increase the employment costs somewhat, notwithstanding the reduction in the growth of wage payments, and thus may lead to a reduction in employment levels over time. However, as in the case of mandated benefits, the reduction in the growth of wage levels will tend to moderate the reduction in employment levels.

COMPARISONS BETWEEN THE ECONOMICS OF TAXATION AND REGULATION

There is an area within the literature of economics in which employment effects are treated explicitly: the literature on the economics of taxation. This literature is directly relevant to the analysis of the employment effects of regulation because: (1) it contains generalized models of the determinants of wage and employment levels, and (2) the causal mechanisms by which taxes and regulations affect wage and employment levels are the same. The mode of analysis that is customarily used for studying the effects of taxation, which economists call "general equilibrium" analysis (described later) is equally applicable—in principle—to regulation. However, to date this mode of analysis has been applied to regulation in only three studies involving only two kinds of regulation. Each of these is discussed later.

In a world without taxes, the cost to employers of hiring an additional hour of labor services and the benefit to a worker of working an additional hour would be the same. As a result of taxes, however, the cost to employers of hiring an additional employee or an additional hour of labor services is greater than the reward received by the employee. In addition to their employees' wages, employers must pay payroll taxes, provide various government-mandated benefits, satisfy paperwork requirements, and so on. Likewise, the net wages received by employees are reduced by federal, state, and local income taxes, and by the employee's share of Social Security.

The total difference between the gross cost incurred by the employer and the net reward received by the employee, after all taxes, is commonly called the "tax wedge." Any tax increase will increase the size of this wedge, causing the gross cost faced by the employer to rise and the net wage received by the employee to fall. Although the balance between gross wage increases and net wage reductions depends on the circumstances, both the demand for labor and the supply of labor will be diminished as a result of an increase in the size of the tax wedge. Conversely, if the size of the tax wedge is reduced, gross hiring costs to firms will fall while net rewards to workers will rise; labor supply, labor demand, and equilibrium labor employment will all rise.[16]

Although the idea of the "wedge" as the difference between gross employment costs to firms and net rewards to workers for working is normally formulated with reference to taxation, it is equally applicable to regulation. As noted in Miles (1984), "Regulation is equivalent to a tax on the activity it governs. Like a tax, regulation drives a wedge between the gross price charged and the net return received by the labor and the capital which generate the activity."

Regulation as much as taxation contributes to the size of the wedge. Just as there is not a multiplicity of wedges with a distinct wedge for each individual tax, there is only a single wedge composed of all taxes acting in unison; so likewise, there are not two separate wedges—one for taxes and one for regulation —but only a single wedge, the total size of which is a function of all taxes and all regulations operating simultaneously. The only thing that matters is the *total* difference between gross wages paid and net wages received. Thus, the nature of the standard mode of analysis used for taxation actually *requires* one to take account of all taxes and regulations simultaneously. On a theoretical level, this mode of analysis is incapable, *in principle*, of treating individual regulations or taxes separately.

The impact of regulations has normally been overlooked in empirical studies using this type of analysis. This has been due to the difficulties of incorporating regulation *in practice* using this type of analysis. The literature on taxation effects now relies almost exclusively on generalized models of the entire economy, called "general equilibrium" models. Those models are discussed in greater detail in Chapter 4.

Similar comprehensive analyses of regulation's effects on the economy as a whole are few and fragmentary. General equilibrium models have so far been applied to regulation in three studies involving two kinds of regulation. Studies by Jorgenson and Wilcoxen (1989, 1990) (unpublished and published versions of the same study) and Hazilla and Kopp (1990) apply computational general equilibrium models to environmental regulation. Another study by Jorgenson and Slesnick (1987)[17] applies a computational general equilibrium model to natural gas price regulation. Only the study by Hazilla and Kopp explicitly considered employment effects. The other two studies deal with aggregate output and consumer welfare, measured in dollars, but do not consider employment levels. Moreover, neither of the latter studies dealing with environmental regulation attempts to take account of the benefits of such regulation.

CONCLUSION

Although new information is coming to light on the employment effects of government intervention in the economy, this issue has still not been addressed adequately in regulatory analyses. The employment effects of regulation are often central to public policy debates on government's role in the economy and in improvement of industrial competitiveness and will continue to be so in the near future. The lack of literature on this issue has somewhat slowed the ability of the government to account for these generally negative impacts in the regulatory decision-making process, as is described in the next chapter.

NOTES

1. Weidenbaum (1980), Hahn (1990), Hanke and Walters (1990) and Weidenbaum (1992) present broad overviews of regulation but do not give any figures for the total cost of regulation. Warren and Lis (1992) presents the total budgetary cost of administering all federal regulations and the total number of employees engaged in writing or enforcing federal regulations.

2. The leading study is Peltzman (1973). See also, e.g., Hanke and Walters (1990), Kazman (1990), Rubin (1992).

3. All of the foregoing figures have been restated in 1988 dollars, as presented by Hahn and Hird (1991), at pp. 255–258.

4. Hopkins (1992) is an abridged version of Hopkins (1991); Hahn and Hopkins (1992) is simply a short synopsis of Hopkins (1991) and Hahn and Hird (1991).

5. This figure was obtained from Hopkins in a telephone conversation with Nancy Bord on June 28, 1992.

6. Specifically, Bord and Laffer (1992) estimate the costs of reserve requirements, deposit insurance, and overall regulatory paperwork and compliance expenditures, but they do not account for the costs of geographic restrictions; restrictions on banks' products, services, and investments; or minimum capital requirements.

7. Bord and Laffer (1992). In their calculations, the wealth transfers that result from economic regulation were counted as costs but were also subtracted as benefits.

8. Bord and Laffer (1992), at p. 13.

9. See, e.g., Bartel and Thomas (1987), Gray (1987, 1991), Hazilla and Kopp (1990), Jorgenson and Wilcoxen (1989, 1990).

10. The one exception is Denison (1985), which found the effects of regulation to be rather modest.

11. Although an increase in the minimum wage may induce a substitution out of low-skilled labor into capital as well as into medium-skilled labor, the higher level of capital employment will not be good per se. Although the additional capital employed may make all classes of labor somewhat more productive, ceteris paribus, the productivity gains due to greater capital employment will necessarily be less than the productivity losses due to the employment of an inferior mix of capital and labor. If a combination involving less low-skilled labor but more medium-skilled labor and more capital would be more conducive to overall productivity growth over time, businesses would have chosen it without any government interference. However, just like any other factor, capital is subject to diminishing returns: both its own marginal product and its incremental contribution to the marginal product of other factors tend to diminish as the quantity of capital employed increases. Moreover, the specific capital that would be added in response to a distortive policy such as an increase in the minimum wage would necessarily be of a lesser quality because it would be tailored to production utilizing a suboptimal factor mix (i.e., too much medium-skilled labor and too little low-skilled labor).

12. See, e.g., Ehrenberg and Smith (1991), Chapter 11 ("The Structure of Compensation"). Because employees normally do not have to pay income tax on their nonwage compensation, they *can* increase the total value of the compensation they receive by taking a portion of their compensation in the form of employer-provided benefits. However, employers who offer their employees this option should be able to succeed in attracting employees with lower wage offers. Thus, the tax savings that result from the provision of compensation in kind normally end up being shared with the employer.

13. See, e.g., Donohue (1986, 1987, 1992), Leonard (1984), Heckman and Payner (1989). Other articles and books dealing with the effectiveness of employment discrimination laws are listed in the Topical Bibliography of Studies on the Effects of Regulation.

14. Posner (1987), Epstein (1992), Bord and Laffer (1992).

15. See, e.g., Ehrenberg and Smith (1991), Chapter 8 ("Compensating Wage Differentials in Labor Markets").

16. The classic exposition is Harberger (1974). See also Canto, Joines and Laffer (1983), Laffer (1981, 1984), Canto (1983), Joines (1983), and Evans (1983).

17. See also Jorgenson and Slesnick (1985).

How Employment Effects Are Addressed in the Regulatory Development Process

The initial point for consideration of the employment effects of a particular regulation is the regulatory development process. Although all federal regulatory agencies interpret legislation, promulgate regulations and administrative guidelines, and ensure that their rules are adhered to, the agencies follow different procedures to develop their regulations. They rarely determine the employment impact of individual rules, groups of rules, or the entire set of federal rules and regulations. Regulations are not viewed or reviewed as part of broadly conceived, coherent programs to achieve particular goals. Rather, they reflect attempts to make specific rules to implement narrow congressional mandates.

This chapter begins with a discussion of the standard tools and techniques that are used to conduct regulatory analysis. It then describes the federal regulatory development process. Finally, several administrative considerations in the regulatory development and review process are examined, using the practical experience of federal agencies that promulgate regulations that affect employment.

STANDARD TOOLS AND TECHNIQUES FOR CONDUCTING REGULATORY ANALYSIS

The analytical approaches and methods used in the regulatory development and review process have evolved over the past several decades. Analytical methods have progressed from what was essentially informal analyses in the early years of regulation to input-output models in the 1970s to the increasing refinements in cost/benefit techniques throughout the 1980s and early 1990s.

As has been noted, an unintended consequence of attempts to achieve important social and safety goals through regulation is the increasing burden on America's economic growth and global competitiveness. Regulators and regulatory decision makers have relied increasingly on economists and other technicians for assistance, believing that more precise and detailed analysis during the regulatory development and review process would help to identify the most significant areas of cost resulting from regulation. In turn, this might ultimately make it possible to design regulation that is less onerous, yet equally or more effective.

Seven tools and techniques are currently used in studying the effects of regulation. Some of these approaches attempt to anticipate the likely effects of regulation; others attempt to measure effects after regulation has been imposed. The seven approaches are

- cost studies
- industry surveys
- engineering studies
- mathematical programming
- econometric estimates
- macroeconomic analysis
- general equilibrium models

These approaches and techniques represent a variety of disciplines. They also differ according to the unit of analysis to which they are applied, the degree to which they are comprehensive and dynamic, the type and amount of data required, and the type and rigor of their results.[1] For example, particular analytical methods and tools are more appropriate to certain types of policy analysis. For example, cost/benefit techniques (along with their many refinements) may be appropriate tools if the focus in regulatory review is on a very specific rule-by-rule basis. However, consideration of the cumulative and more comprehensive effects of potential regulations requires analytical tools and techniques more suitable to capturing these broad effects. The seven approaches are summarized in the following chart.

The two most important criteria for evaluating the relative strengths of the respective tools and techniques are their comprehensiveness and their ability to predict the effects of a regulation's imposition.

First, the tools and techniques should be capable of assessing a regulation's effects both on the enterprises that are the intended targets of the regulation and on the entire economy; likewise, tools are needed that can address regulatory programs as a whole. Although such tools already exist, they are rarely applied in regulatory development and review at present.

A related problem with comprehensiveness is whether the tool or technique allows for the substitutability of labor for other factors of production. If the price of labor increases, a profit-maximizing firm will look for ways to use more capital-intensive techniques. This change in technology might take the form of simply replacing several secretaries on typewriters with an efficient word processor, or

SUMMARY OF
TOOLS AND TECHNIQUES FOR REGULATORY ANALYSIS

cost studies

measure the overall costs of regulations that have been placed on an economy at a particular point in time

industry surveys

measure the effects of regulation on a particular industry rather than on an economy in general

engineering studies

examine the impacts of regulation on particular enterprises and production processes, generally after a regulation is in place

mathematical programming

predict or anticipate the likely effects of regulation on a given process or series of processes

econometric estimates

predict the cost effects of a regulation on an industry, if the regulation is focused on a particular industry, or on the economy as a whole, if the regulation is to be applied generally

macroeconomic analysis

focus on trends over a number of years throughout the economy in an attempt to show the effects of regulations on a specific factor or set of factors

general equilibrium models

measure or predict the effects of different government policies on many aspects of an economy's activities by relying on a model of an entire economy's functioning several clerks with a computer-automated billing system. Of course, sectors differ in their ability to substitute labor for other factors in this way. For example, service sectors tend to have a high degree of substitutability compared to the manufacturing or mining sector. These differences can be important for measuring the employment impacts of regulations to the extent that regulations affect sectors differently.

Second, the tools and techniques used in regulatory analysis should be able to predict the likely impact of regulations on a broad scale before the regulations come into force. Tools and techniques that can only assess effects after regulations are in place, or can only take into account effects at the process or enterprise level, are less useful to regulatory decision makers.

Engineering studies, mathematical programming, econometric estimates, and general equilibrium models can be used to predict effects of a regulation's imposition. However, the first three tools all tend to be limited to one industry or sector of the economy and do not capture the effects of one sector of the economy on all other sectors. As such, they are not suited to studying the effects of regulation on the economy as a whole. For example, if some regulatory policy were expected to reduce the demand for low-sulfur coal, then those tools and techniques would be used to estimate employment impacts on the coal industry. No impacts on employment in sectors that *used* coal as an input would be studied.

Engineering studies, mathematical programming, and econometric estimates also fail to capture the cumulative effects of regulation over time on savings, investment, capital formation, and technological change.

In contrast, general equilibrium models permit simulation of the effects of various regulatory proposals on an entire economy and over different periods. (Although they generally do not pick up changes in technology over time, computational general equilibrium [CGE] models hold technology [or its rate of change] constant for purposes of studying effects on output, employment, and welfare.) Nevertheless, like those of econometric models, the results yielded by general equilibrium models depend heavily on the parameters and assumptions that are built into the model.

Cost Studies

Studies of the costs of regulation in general, or of a particular regulation or category of regulation, are the most frequently used and the most widely publicized in regulatory analysis. Cost studies attempt to measure (i.e., quantify) the overall costs and effects of regulations that have been placed on an economy at a particular time. They may not consider all possible costs, depending on the availability of data (several specific methods of attempting to measure costs are discussed in the following subsections), and they sometimes do not use rigorous statistical techniques.

Cost studies may sometimes consider offsetting benefits, though most do not. Benefits are even more difficult to measure because the beneficiaries of regulation do not (and often cannot) indicate the value they attach to the benefits by purchasing them in the market.

Industry Surveys

Industry surveys are similar to cost studies, except that they focus on the effects of regulation on a particular industry rather than on the economy in general. Industry studies are usually performed after a regulation has gone into effect and measure the impacts on the industry at a particular time.

These studies of particular industry impacts generally require that specific data be collected from the industry or from industry associations. Industry surveys can differ widely in the degree of rigor employed in their analysis. Organized industry groups with a particular focus often undertake such surveys for their members and for the purpose of influencing the policy process. As a result, there is sometimes a danger that such surveys will overstate the costs of regulations that the firms in an industry would like to prevent or have removed.

Engineering Studies

Engineering studies examine the impacts of regulation on particular enterprises and production processes, generally after a regulation is in place. A high degree of statistical rigor characterizes these studies because engineering analysis tends to be quite precise. The data required are particular to the enterprise and the process being studied.

Engineering studies are useful to managers of enterprises having highly regulated production processes, involving complicated scientific and technical equipment or materials. They are likely to address health, safety, or environmental concerns.

Mathematical Programming

Mathematical programming studies of regulatory effects are related to engineering studies in some respects. Whereas engineering studies assess the effects on enterprises and production processes after regulations affecting them have been promulgated, mathematical programming studies attempt to predict or anticipate the likely effects of regulation on a given process or series of processes. Production and operating managers find these types of analyses useful for adapting to regulations affecting their activities. These studies are more flexible and dynamic than studies using the cost study, industry survey, or engineering approach, in that the use of operations research tools permits simulation of alternative effects and levels of impact.

Econometric Estimates

Econometric estimation of regulatory effects is being used increasingly in the formal Regulatory Impact Analyses (RIAs) conducted by U.S. government agencies. RIAs are required as a component of the regulatory review process for major regulations, except for those regulations that are statutorily exempt from review by congressional action. Economists in universities, government agencies, or consulting firms are most likely to employ econometric estimation in their contribution to the regulatory review process.

Econometric estimates are undertaken to attempt to predict the cost effects of a regulation on an industry, if the regulation is focused on a particular industry, or on the economy as a whole, if the regulation is to be applied generally. The data needed for such analyses depend upon the number and types of estimates to be made. Estimates derived by using standard econometric techniques are likely to have a high level of statistical rigor. However, the accuracy of these estimates will depend heavily on the quality of the underlying data and the accuracy of the assumptions underlying the econometric model employed. The precision resulting from sophisticated statistical techniques does not guarantee that the results will be accurate in measuring or predicting the cost effects of a regulation because of the assumptions employed and data limitations.

Macroeconomic Analysis

Studies of the effects of regulation on macroeconomic factors such as gross domestic product (GDP), capital flows, and trade patterns are generally undertaken after regulations are in effect. These studies focus on the entire economy, and they tend to focus on trends over a number of years in an attempt to show the effects of regulations on a specific factor or set of factors. For example, studies of the effects of regulation on GDP or trade flows have been increasingly common in recent years. The data requirements for such analyses are high, but data on most macro factors are easy to obtain. Policy analysts and economic researchers are most likely to employ these techniques to assess the positive and negative effects of regulation.

General Equilibrium Models

General models of an entire economy's functioning, which economists call "general equilibrium" models, can be used to measure or predict the effects of different government policies, including taxes and regulations, on many aspects of an economy's activities. Such models not only are comprehensive in scope but also are flexible and dynamic.

The current state of the art in this area is represented by computational general equilibrium (CGE) models. These models, which are very complicated and difficult to design and develop, are the methodological offspring of the input-output models of the 1960s and 1970s. CGE models are basically a large set of demand and supply functions that cover every market, for both commodities and factors of production.

As many regulators typically focus only on the particular industry that they regulate, the overall, economywide impacts of the regulations on employment in other industries can be easily overlooked. Even if a regulation applies to one or a few sectors, there will likely be important employment effects in other sectors due to the interconnections among sectors. Therefore, the use of economywide models to assess economywide employment effects is essential. This is particularly important because so many recent regulations in the areas of health, safety, environment, and civil rights apply to all sectors of the economy.

A number of their characteristics give CGE models an advantage over alternative methods that do not examine economywide impacts or allow for any factor substitution by firms. There is a substantial consensus among commentators on the regulatory process that macro models are the tools best able to address economywide concerns.[2] These approaches also permit assessment of the cumulative effects of regulatory programs rather than merely addressing specific rules.

CGE models can incorporate both macroeconomic and microeconomic variables and processes, and are among the best tools for addressing economywide concerns from the point of view of ensuring as complete and rigorous consideration of the employment and wage effects of regulation as is currently possible. CGE models are sometimes confused with traditional macro models because they can encompass the entire economy, but they should not be, since traditional macro models lack the CGE model's dynamic properties and ability to identify indirect effects.

The use of CGE models in the evaluation of broader regulatory programs has been limited. They are costly and require a considerable amount of time to develop, and they require specially skilled individuals to operate them and, more importantly, to interpret their results.

THE REGULATORY DEVELOPMENT PROCESS

The regulatory development process can be extremely complex, depending upon the number and variety of participants. Who participates is, in turn, a function of the regulation itself and its scope and complexity. Another variable in the process is whether Congress has mandated specific requirements or a schedule for regulatory review, or whether the agency assigned to prepare a regulation has discretion in these matters. For example, rules or standards pertaining only to a single industry or to a single process, operation, or substance are likely to involve fewer participants, both inside and outside government, and to take less time to prepare than regulations that apply to many industries or to many processes, operations, or substances.

Increasingly, Congress has been including time constraints for regulatory preparation and review in the underlying legislation for which implementing regulations or standards are to be prepared. No matter what the time frame, the formal framework established by the Administrative Procedure Act (APA) of 1946 (5 U.S.C. § 553) stipulates that certain steps must be taken and in a specified order. That legislation describes a multistep process that has constituted the basic framework for agency practices. In general, each of the major regulatory agencies has a formal protocol for developing, promulgating, and enforcing its guidelines, regulations, standards, and administrative decisions.

The steps in the rulemaking process (which are presented here in a boilerplate mode) begin with the enactment by Congress of legislation which, in turn, requires specific rules and regulations for its implementation. Rules and regulations are drafted by the federal agency designated by Congress. In conducting its analyses, the agency will utilize some of the tools and techniques discussed previously in this chapter. A "notice of proposed rule making" or "NPRM" is published in the *Federal Register*, which notifies interested parties of the proposed rule and permits a period for public comment on it.

A proposed rule is also reviewed internally by various units of the agency in question, and sometimes by other government agencies as well. After the agency has reviewed and revised the proposal, in light of the public comments and its own internal review, the proposed rule is sent to the Office of Management and Budget (OMB). The Office of Information and Regulatory Affairs (OIRA) and its predecessors in OMB and the Executive Office of the President (such as the Council on Wage and Price Stability) have been responsible for regulatory review at the White House level. It is through this agency, theoretically insulated from the normal dynamics of the political process, that broad changes in regulatory procedures can most easily occur.

At OMB, the proposed rule is reviewed by OIRA and then returned to the agency with OIRA's recommendations. Discussions between OMB and the agency may lead to changes in the rule. The final version of the rule is then published in the *Federal Register* and, after taking effect, enforced by the appropriate agency.

In the decades following enactment of the APA, Congress passed many laws that included rule-making procedures, guidelines, and specific requirements to supplement or, in some cases, supersede the provisions of the APA. In addition, the increasing complexity and controversial nature of regulation sometimes required agencies to modify their rule-making procedures to comply with judicial mandates. In fact, some agencies may follow different rule-making procedures for different laws under their jurisdiction.

A significant addition to the regulatory development and review process was Executive Order (EO) 12291, which required agencies to inquire into the overall benefits and costs of proposed regulations. Issued by President Reagan in 1981, EO 12291 required executive branch agencies to weigh the costs and benefits of proposed regulations. However, because costs and benefits can take different forms in different contexts, the meanings and applications of the terms "cost" and "benefit" can vary depending on the agency and type of regulation involved. Furthermore, some regulatory areas, such as those affecting the military, were exempt from EO 12291's cost/benefit analysis requirements.

There has not, however, been any executive order specifically requiring the assessment of a proposed regulation's effects on employment, although employment effects may be interpreted by some as included in EO 12291 and EO 12668 (issued by President Clinton). A framework such as that laid out in EO 12291 was important because—absent a specific requirement for consideration of employment effects in the rule-making process—cost/benefit analysis is the principal rubric under which employment effects of proposed regulations are likely to be considered.

ADMINISTRATIVE CONSIDERATIONS IN THE REGULATORY DEVELOPMENT PROCESS

A number of administrative considerations are critical to a regulatory development and review process that incorporates the employment and wage effects of regulation. These considerations include the structure of regulatory institutions within the executive branch, agency practices and procedures, agency resources, and political philosophy.

In order to determine how key federal agencies involved in the regulatory process addressed those considerations as well as the employment effects of proposed regulations, interviews were conducted in 1992 with relevant officials in seven different agencies having primary responsibility for employment-related or employment-affecting regulations. The agencies examined were the

- Department of the Interior
- Department of Justice (Civil Rights Division)
- Department of Labor—Occupational Safety and Health Administration (OSHA)
- Department of Labor—agencies other than OSHA
- Environmental Protection Agency (EPA)

- Equal Employment Opportunity Commission (EEOC)
- National Labor Relations Board (NLRB)

In addition to the interviews, specific impact studies were reviewed from two key agencies that conduct formal regulatory impact analyses—OSHA and EPA.

Those seven agencies were chosen because they account for the major portion of the U.S. federal regulatory burden that is not specific to an industry. The scope of their various regulatory authorities includes the general physical environment (EPA and Interior), the physical working environment (OSHA), and economic and social aspects of the working environment (EEOC, Justice, Labor, and NLRB). OSHA is listed separately from the rest of the Department of Labor because OSHA followed a different set of procedures in its regulatory decision-making process. Their regulations are applicable throughout the private sector and, in the case of EPA and OSHA, to some segments of the public sector. The seven agencies studied differ in terms of how they are organized and staffed, in the procedures that they use to carry out regulatory development and review functions, and in the types and forms of analyses they conduct.

Structure of Regulatory Institutions within the Executive Branch

Staffing complements and the level of organization to which the unit responsible for regulatory review reports varied from agency to agency. The regulatory review units in older, established agencies, such as the Departments of the Interior and Labor, were headed by deputy assistant secretaries. At the Department of Labor, regulatory review had a designated professional staff, whereas at Interior there were no staff specifically designated for this function.

Not surprisingly, the more recently established agencies such as the EEOC, EPA, and OSHA all had formally designated staffs for regulatory development and review. Furthermore, the agencies most frequently involved in formal regulatory review, such as EPA and OSHA, tended to have the most elaborate processes. Since these agencies are not cabinet-level departments, managerial titles differ from the conventional secretary, deputy secretary, and so on. From the various agency organization charts it appears that the directors supervising regulatory review were at a level in the decision-making hierarchy generally equivalent to a deputy assistant secretary. The NLRB, an anomaly since it was precluded by statute from having a formal regulatory review process (other than a legal conflict review), placed responsibility for this activity with the executive secretary, who reports directly to the board.

The composition of the designated staffs and senior management involved in regulatory development and review in the various agencies is another structural factor that affected how regulatory review was carried out and the issues that were considered in a regulatory review. Of the agencies studied, OSHA and EPA had the largest designated regulatory review staffs, as well as the only staffs comprising professional economists who were likely to be familiar with the tools and techniques of rigorous benefit/cost analysis. All other agency staffs were composed primarily of lawyers, who generally were not trained in or focused on the types of economic analysis that may be required to determine the effects of regulation on employment and productivity.

Although the structural factors characterizing most agencies' regulatory development and review processes diminished the likelihood that employment effects would be addressed explicitly and systematically in regulatory review, sometimes there are other participants in the process who may address employment effects. EPA reported regularly involving industry advisers, outside consultants, and other regulatory agencies in its regulatory review process. The EEOC and the Department of Labor both reported frequent use of outside consulting studies, but not necessarily direct involvement of consultants in the regulatory review process. OSHA reported using both industry advisers and outside consultants in regulatory review. The Department of the Interior appeared to be more likely than most other agencies to involve other agencies in its review process.

Agency Practices and Procedures

Agency practices and procedures, both among and within agencies, tended to be highly variable, inconsistent, and frequently conflicting. This tended to be the case even when the activities were directed toward the same objective or were operating under the same congressional mandate or presidential executive order.

The more precise the executive order, and the closer the relationship between the approaches embodied in an executive order and the operating style of the agency, the more likely it was that the executive order's provisions would be carried out in the spirit as well as the letter of the law. This point was demonstrated in a 1992 analysis of agency practices under EO 12291, which found nominal compliance with the formalities of the order but remarkable and widespread disregard for the order's objectives.[3]

Surveying federal agencies' practices for assessing the costs and benefits of regulation revealed a wide variety of patterns and styles. These patterns and styles reflected differences in agency culture and orientation as well as the characteristics of the regulations developed and administered by each agency. Other variables that affected agency practices included agency relationships with external constituencies in the Washington policy matrix, that is, Congress and the executive, special interest groups, and associations concerned with agency practices. In other words, the processes and practices by which a regulation is developed and administered within the agencies are highly politicized despite attempts to make the process more rigorously analytical and insulate it from the political dynamics of Washington.

One school of thought holds that efforts to immunize regulatory development and review from the political process are futile and doomed to failure. By definition, regulatory development and administration are integral parts of the policy process and are inherently political. Others contend that the application of ever more sophisticated tools and techniques in the regulatory review process combined with explicit assessment of potential implications for specific dimensions of economic activity (i.e., employment, small business, federalism) can counter or mitigate the inherently political nature of regulatory development and administration.

A focus on the actual process by which regulations are developed and reviewed prior to promulgation tended to lend credence to some aspects of both views. Again, marked differences were observed among agencies and over time. These fluctuations were influenced by the policy agenda and priorities of Congress and the executive and by the backgrounds, predilections, and career objectives of agency staff.

Four of the agencies (EEOC, EPA, Labor, and OSHA) conducted formal regulatory impact analyses (RIAs) as required by Executive Order 12291. The Justice and Interior Departments' rule making functions were established before the executive orders of the 1970s and 1980s requiring specific factors to be taken into account in regulatory review. The NLRB rarely engaged in rule-making. Furthermore, it was forbidden by statute to undertake economic analyses of its regulatory proposals.

Of the agencies reviewed, only EPA and OSHA regularly performed RIAs and regulatory flexibility analyses (RFAs), designed to assess regulatory impacts specifically on small and medium sized enterprises. Their analyses tended to focus on direct, measurable costs of compliance incurred in particular sectors of the economy, thereby ignoring indirect and social costs. Their studies were narrowly focused, excluding consideration of alternative approaches to achieving regulatory objectives. They rarely considered employment effects explicitly; even when they did, only industry estimates—based on current industry structures, processes and technologies—were given.

The Departments of Labor and the Interior reported conducting less comprehensive industry impact analyses. The Department of Justice and the EEOC reported conducting analyses on a case-by-case basis, since their rule making is often not amenable to comprehensive RIA analysis, and their enforcement of regulation—like that of the NLRB as well—is "complaint-driven." That is, a specific complaint is required in order to trigger the regulatory enforcement process.

The level of detail characterizing each agency's regulatory review analysis was related to the frequency and type of regulation at issue. EPA and OSHA tended to have very detailed, "data-heavy" analyses. The Departments of Justice and the Interior, to the extent that they perform regulatory impact analyses at all, tended to do so with very few specific data. The practices of the EEOC and the Department of Labor with respect to the level of data and detail in regulatory review fell somewhere in between.

None of the surveyed agencies consistently and systematically addressed employment effects of proposed regulations or regulatory enforcement actions. EPA and OSHA sometimes addressed such issues in the context of an RIA study. However, since such studies were usually performed by outside contractors, there was considerable variation in the ways in which employment effects were addressed under the aegis of these agencies.

EPA and OSHA have been responsible for some of the most comprehensive and detailed regulations promulgated by federal agencies. The two agencies are considered to have a substantial impact on the overall costs of regulation to the U.S. economy.[4] Thus, the scope and nature of the RIAs and RFAs undertaken by these two agencies during this period provide insight into the way in which the regulatory review process is carried out. In addition, since the regulations proposed by EPA and OSHA can have such broad and serious implications, whether or not employment effects are considered in these agencies' RIAs—and if so, how—is a significant matter.

The RIA studies were conducted by using the general framework specified by EO 12291. There were significant differences in approach, however. The EPA studies did not consider the option of having no regulation at all, or of using less intrusive, more "market-oriented" regulatory approaches or methods. Rather, they simply compared the projected costs and benefits of setting the proposed regulatory standards at several different levels. The OSHA regulatory impact studies, although rejecting the "no regulation" option as well as all alternative regulatory approaches (including any approaches that would place greater reliance on markets and less on overt regulation), at least alluded to these other possibilities as options.

In conducting the studies, the agencies and their consultants focused on particular industries that would most obviously be affected by the regulations. In some instances, impacts on particular industry segments or products were examined. Impacts were measured in terms of costs likely to be incurred in complying with the proposed standards.

All four of the EPA studies explicitly considered employment effects for particular industry segments. For example, the sulfur dioxide and acid rain standards were shown to be related to the future demand for low-sulfur western coal as opposed to higher-sulfur Appalachian coal. Thus, the EPA's contractors could not help considering the dislocation in coal mining employment patterns likely to occur with these shifts in demand. Similarly, the RIA for the air quality standards for lead concluded that certain industry segments could not comply and still be economically viable. Therefore, job losses due to plant closure had to be considered. A related EPA-sponsored study, which was not an RIA under EO 12291, explored the employment effects of the Clean Air Act Amendments of 1990 in terms of job creation in the pollution control industry. Both OSHA studies only briefly alluded to employment effects and did not examine them in any detail.

The principal methods and analytical techniques used in the EPA and OSHA studies reflected the requirements of the agencies involved. Econometric estimates are frequently used to estimate costs and benefits in these analyses. The results produced by these techniques tended to show a high degree of precision and statistical validity. However, precision and accuracy are not the same, although they are often confused. For example, the fact that the cost of a particular regulation may be calculated to nine or eleven decimal places (i.e., if the regulation in question costs at least one billion dollars, to the nearest dollar or penny) does not make the number accurate or correct. If the calculation is based on faulty data or assumptions, the number may be off by several orders of magnitude. And yet, the inclusion of so many figures to the right of the decimal point may give the number the appearance of accuracy.

Many models are based on assumptions that are dubious at best. Moreover, these models frequently omit any variables for which statistical data bases are not readily available—regardless of the importance of the omitted variables to the issues the models examine. Yet, because of the apparent precision and statistical validity these models possess, many people in policy-making roles in the bureaucracy and Congress simply accept their results without question.

OMB's regulatory review arm, OIRA, scrutinized agency regulations. During the Reagan and Bush administrations, OMB/OIRA critiques of regulatory impact analyses increasingly faulted agencies for failure to assess benefits, as well as for inadequate data and slipshod or inadequately rigorous methods in preparing cost estimates. OMB had been particularly critical of RIAs prepared by or for EPA and OSHA.

Agency Resources

Resources (time, budget, and quantity and quality of personnel) also varied dramatically among the agencies. Thus, incorporating assessment of employment effects into the regulatory review process must deal with this administrative reality. Agencies' regulatory review functions differ in terms of the time available for review because, as noted earlier, Congress has increasingly sought to limit agency discretion in rule making by imposing strict time limits on certain regulatory tasks. As might be expected, the more politically sensitive Congress considers a regulation to be, the tighter the mandated schedule to promulgate the regulation.

A case in point is the Americans with Disabilities Act, which required literally thousands of regulations to be prepared by nearly a dozen agencies within nine to twelve of the legislation's passage. It is appearing more and more likely that some of the regulations prepared under this act were not carefully considered or carefully drafted in a way that minimizes their potentially burdensome impact on small business, as required under the Regulatory Flexibility Act of 1980 (P.L. 96–354).

As for differences in the financial resources available to regulatory agencies, budget making and appropriations to agencies are functions of Congress, but disbursement is the responsibility of the executive. Simply by adjusting either one of these elements, an agency's resources, and hence its ability to carry out its regulatory activities, can be profoundly affected. The experience of the Antitrust Division of the Justice Department during the Reagan administration illustrated this point. The decline in antitrust actions brought by the department resulted not only from an ideological orientation of Reagan appointees, but also from a corresponding lack of funds and personnel to pursue such actions.

Agencies differed in terms of the number and quality of their staffs, both political appointees and career civil servants. When the quality of both is high and the agency is in favor with both Congress and the executive, constructive action may be more likely. However, this is rarely the case, and, as a consequence, administrative coherence is likely to give way to internal dissension over the details of procedures. The ability of agency staffs to modify regulatory development and review procedures is also a factor to be considered, especially if new procedures involve the use of more sophisticated analytical tools or techniques. If more sophisticated tools and techniques are a component of regulatory development and review, it is critical that agency staffs be capable of using them.

Finally, the close working relationships developed over time between key agency staff and congressional office and committee staff, and their effect on agency activities, have been well documented and represent another administrative reality to be acknowledged in assessing regulatory development and review.[5] Executive agencies have external constituencies, many of which are highly organized and resource-rich, which are interested in and knowledgeable about specific regulatory areas.

Political Philosophy

Whether agency practices regarding regulatory development and review are likely to change when a new administration with a different regulatory philosophy takes office depends in large part upon the statutory structure that is in place, including executive orders governing regulatory review, and on personnel changes in key executive agency supervisory roles and at OMB and OIRA.

When the Clinton administration assumed office, for example, there was less change initially then might have been expected given that the Clinton administration appeared to subscribe to the notion that more government involvement in all aspects of economic and social life is a "good thing," and that federal regulation is a principal means of ensuring this. Most accounts now reflect an accelerated pace of regulatory action that harkens back to the 1970s. However, the Bush administration presided over a significant increase in regulation despite the rhetoric to the contrary, as many commentators have noted. During the Bush administration, Congress enacted, and the president signed, the 1990 Clean Air Act Amendments and the Americans with Disabilities Act, among other measures that expanded the scope and reach of federal regulation of business.

The issues of legal structure and personnel changes assume greater importance in assessing the likely direction of regulation. As a corollary, the extent to which agency practices for regulatory development and review are substantially modified when a new administration takes office is often limited by basic agency dynamics and the fact that the vast majority of regulatory development and review functions are carried out by career civil servants.

CONCLUSION

The models and methods currently used in regulatory analyses are less than adequate to deal fully, rigorously, and systematically with the employment effects of regulation. Similarly, regulatory review practices in the seven key federal regulatory agencies surveyed generally did not explicitly or systematically take all potential employment effects into consideration during the review process or in enforcement decisions. Even in those rare instances when employment effects were considered, they were considered only in terms of the general category of "employee," making no distinctions among skill levels or functions.

More comprehensive methods and models could enhance the tools currently available to federal regulatory agencies in the regulatory development and review process, particularly pertaining to the consideration of employment effects. Such methods and models could include, but not necessarily be limited to, a framework based on a generalized model of the economy. The next chapter addresses how a higher level of analysis has been applied at the level of the White House and the Executive Office of the President.

NOTES

1. This framework for comparing analytical tools and techniques is adapted from Bord (1969). A similar framework is set out in Hahn and Hird (1991).

2. See, e.g., Bord (1992); Bord and Laffer (1992), at p. 11; Hazilla and Kopp (1990), pp. 853–873; Crandall (1992), at pp. 2–4. But see Hahn and Hird (1991), at pp. 244–246, enumerating both the advantages and disadvantages of general equilibrium models, and concluding that the disadvantages sometimes can outweigh the advantages, depending on the circumstances.

3. David Wojick et al., study prepared for Citizens for a Sound Economy, August 1992.

4. See, e.g., Bartel and Thomas (1985, 1987), Gray (1987, 1991), Hopkins (1991) (pp.

11–12 and table 2), Hazilla and Kopp (1990), and Jorgenson and Wilcoxen (1989, 1990).

    5. See, e.g., "America's Parasite Economy," *The Economist*, October 10, 1992; Miller, James C. III and Philip Mink, "The Ink of the Octopus," *Policy Review*, Summer 1992.

The Regulatory Review Process

Accompanying the growth in federal government regulation of the economy over the past twenty-five years has been a formal regulatory review process that was developed to ensure (1) a measure of coordination and coherence among regulators, and (2) consideration of the economic implications of regulation. In fact, it is at the regulatory review stage of the process (rather than the regulatory development stage discussed in the last chapter) that we have seen the most activity concerning the costs and benefits of regulation for the economy, as well as the employment effects of regulation.

Understanding the current regulatory review process and its evolution is essential in designing a plan that improves the consideration of employment effects. This chapter begins with a discussion of policy issues important to the regulatory review process, and then focuses on the role of Presidential intervention in that process over the past twenty years and the legal/judicial basis for that intervention.

POLICY CONSIDERATIONS IN REGULATORY REVIEW

Characteristics of the overall policy context in which regulatory review occurs can influence the choice of suitable and feasible approaches for regulatory analysis and specifically for addressing of employment effects in the regulatory review process. Fundamental features of U.S. policy-making institutions and their relationships can encourage or impede the adoption and effective implementation of such approaches.

Key cases in recent administrative law, touching upon regulatory policy (noted in the previous section), are involved with delineating the respective powers of the executive represented by agencies reporting to the chief executive, and the legislature, in terms of activities specifically delegated to executive agencies through legislation. The inherent tension between the two branches of the federal government invites participation of the third branch—the judiciary—to resolve conflicts between the branches as they manifest themselves in the regulatory process.

Another aspect of the policy context relevant to addressing employment effects in the regulatory process involves the dominant regulatory philosophy, or contending regulatory philosophies, of the moment. The regulatory philosophy of policymakers in either Congress or the executive branch mattered less when regulation was less pervasive and less burdensome to the economy, and the regulatory process was simpler and less institutionalized, as in the 1960s. However, the decision makers' regulatory philosophy does matter now that regulation is a major public policy concern, at federal, state, and local levels.

As a result of the 1994 election, observers are watching as regulatory agencies seek to balance the aggressive regulatory policy of the Clinton administration with the free market approach promoted by the Republican Congress. There has been some give-and-take on both sides, as regulatory agencies have pursued actions to streamline the regulatory process and Republican legislators have seen some of their most strident attempts at redefining regulation rebuffed by coalitions composed of moderate Republicans and Democrats.

The dominant regulatory philosophy of an administration can be inferred (even if it is not explicitly enunciated in executive orders) from the chronology of formal rules, policy foci, and types of tools and techniques used in regulatory policy analysis. A new presidential administration can articulate a change in regulatory philosophy, extending even to review procedures. However, there are times when its room to maneuver is circumscribed by the highly elaborate regulatory process, supported by interests in Congress, the agencies, and nongovernmental special interest groups.

A new administration can, of course, dismantle an existing review structure by rescinding executive orders, and so forth, but the intrinsic dynamics of the regulatory process dictate that something else must be put in its place. Given the tremendous burden of regulation on the economy, it is not likely that any administration would abandon at least the semblance of rigorous economic analysis in the regulatory review process. If the executive does not do so, Congress certainly will.

THE PRESIDENTIAL ROLE IN REGULATORY REVIEW

The elaboration of the formal framework for regulatory review has been accompanied by a shifting policy focus. Aside from nominating appointees to federal regulatory agencies, presidential intervention in the regulatory process during the first two phases of federal regulation (see Chapter 2) focused primarily on issues of coordination. The concern was on eliminating duplication of effort and overlap among agencies. Frequent duplication of regulation during this period stemmed from the fact that most regulations were promulgated by regulatory agencies "independent" of the executive branch of government.

More recently, agencies that shared or experienced overlapping jurisdictions relied upon institutions such as interagency committees and task forces, and instruments such as memoranda of understanding, to coordinate regulatory activities and resolve their differences. One example was the Interagency Regulatory Liaison Group, a Carter administration committee set up to coordinate regulatory actions on chemicals in the environment by the EPA, OSHA, the Food and Drug Administration, and the Consumer Product Safety Commission.

Prior to 1970, when regulation was primarily economic and applicable to specific industries, its overall effect on the economy was less visible than today. There was little need for a formal regulatory review process. Most regulatory reviews took place either informally before a regulation was promulgated or by challenges in the courts after it was promulgated.

During the 1970s, the policy approach to regulatory review, both in Congress and in the executive agencies, expanded from a focus on specific regulatory programs to the broader social and economic implications of regulatory actions. The passage of the National Environmental Policy Act in 1969 and the Occupational Health and Safety Act in 1970 dramatically changed the nature of regulation in the United States. Regulation became comprehensive and applicable to all industry or commercial sectors, rather than specific to a particular industry. Post-1970 regulation tended to be directed toward social, rather than economic, goals (although it is recognized that there were and are significant economic ramifications to pursuing social goals via regulation).

Disagreements among regulators became increasingly difficult to resolve at the agency level. When agencies could not resolve issues among themselves, they sought presidential involvement in the process.

In recent history, regulatory reviews occurred at three points. At the agency level, administrative officers in agencies perform regulatory review tasks as indicated under the Administrative Procedure Act (APA) of 1946, the current presidential executive order on regulation (which is, at present, EO 12866), and the Regulatory Flexibility Act, which requires that special consideration be given to differential impacts of regulation on small businesses. The second point in the review process is the Office of Information and Regulatory Affairs (OIRA) in the Office of Management and Budget (OMB) in the Executive Office of the President. The third point of review has occurred historically at the White House level. That role was filled by the Council on Competitiveness (located in the Office of the Vice President) during the Bush administration; most regulatory decisions in the Clinton administration occur at the OMB level.

During this period, Congress increased its concern over the independent status of most regulatory agencies. This concern has been seen in the increased level of public debate and contention between the legislative and executive branches over the president's role in regulatory review.[1] At the same time, greater attention was paid to the procedures utilized in regulatory development; more parties both inside and outside government became interested in and affected by regulation and the regulatory process.

Since the institution of the "quality of life" reviews that were put in place during the Nixon administration, presidents have instituted increasingly sophisticated analytical tools and review procedures to assess and control regulatory costs. However, White House and agency attempts to determine accurately the costs and benefits of regulation for the economy (including the employment impacts) have been inconsistent and imprecise. White House regulatory reviews often occurred late in the regulatory process, almost as a stopgap measure for runaway regulators, rather than being part of a logical and comprehensive process.

Ford Administration

Most formal regulatory analyses prior to 1980 were conducted because of concerns about what was then thought to be a spiraling rate of inflation. President Nixon had instituted economywide wage and price controls in August 1971. One of the agencies involved in reviewing the gradual elimination of price controls during the 1970s was the Council on Wage and Price Stability (CWPS). The Council on Wage and Price Stability Act (P.L. 93–387, as amended) directed CWPS, to, inter alia, "intervene and otherwise participate in rule making, ratemaking, licensing, and other proceedings . . . in order to present its views [on] the inflationary impact that might result from the possible outcomes of such proceedings."

President Ford's EO 11821 (November 27, 1974) required that all executive branch departments and agencies prepare an Inflation Impact Statement (IIS) for proposals that were expected to have a major impact on consumers, business, and employment. These economic analyses, to be prepared for all major regulations, had to contain completed analyses of the costs, benefits, and alternatives associated with a regulation before that regulation was published in the *Federal Register*. If the costs exceeded the benefits, the proposal was classified as inflationary. If the benefits were greater than the costs, the regulation was classified as noninflationary. OMB was given overall responsibility for implementing the executive order, and was given the specific responsibility of reviewing legislatively mandated IISs. CWPS evaluated IISs on other proposed rules and regulations.

In EO 11949 (December 1976), President Ford directed agencies to conduct Economic Impact Analyses (in lieu of IISs) of major regulations. CWPS was directed to ensure that these EIAS were conducted.

An important regulatory issue is the tension between executive privilege and public accountability in the regulatory review process. In 1976, Congress sought to address that issue and increase the transparency of agency decision making by passing the Government in the Sunshine Act of 1976.

Carter Administration

Despite the Ford administration's efforts to assess the implications of regulation, the business community pursued the cost burden of federal regulations as a major policy issue for the incoming Carter administration. In response to the business community's concerns, the issues of regulation and regulatory reform occupied a prominent place in that administration.

The Carter administration had two goals for its regulatory reform program. The first was to deregulate those markets where government intervention had restricted competition needlessly and produced no benefit to the general welfare. Major deregulation efforts were initiated for airlines, banking, crude oil and natural gas, trucking, and railroads.

The second goal was to improve the management of needed regulatory programs. The administration's regulatory improvement program focused largely on regulatory review, relying upon the diverse tools of executive orders and review and coordination agencies.

President Carter issued EO 12044 ("Improving Government Regulations," March 23, 1978), which required all federal agencies to conduct economic impact analyses of their proposed regulations, whenever those regulations may have a substantial impact on the economy. Agencies were directed to prepare a regulatory analysis for each major rule, assessing its economic effects and alternate means of achieving its objectives, among other things. The executive order stated that regulations "shall not impose unnecessary burdens on the economy, on individuals, on public or private organizations, or on state and local governments." When signing EO 12044, Carter said "This executive order . . . directs that whenever a regulation may have a major economic consequence, the agency must conduct an early and rigorous examination of all alternatives of achieving a stated objective." A second executive order (EO 12174, November 30, 1979) addressed paperwork reduction. A third executive order (EO 12221, June 27, 1980) extended the expiration date of EO 12044 until April 30, 1981.

OMB was designated to oversee agency compliance with the key management and procedural reforms required under EO 12044. OMB established an Office of Regulatory and Information Policy to handle its responsibilities for regulatory policy, reports management, and information policy, as well as the executive orders on regulation and paperwork.

Most regulatory analyses, however, were conducted by CWPS. From its creation in 1974 until its demise in 1981, CWPS intervened in over three hundred rule-making and rate-making proceedings. In matters of economic regulation, CWPS encouraged reductions in entry and pricing restrictions in such areas as transportation, banking, agriculture, and energy. CWPS required that regulations be based on the best obtainable evidence of the costs and benefits of alternative strategies.

Yet, the agency most visibly involved in regulatory review during the Carter administration was the Regulatory Analysis Review Group (RARG). RARG was established by President Carter to assist individual agencies in meeting the goals of EO 12044 and to review and comment on selected regulatory analyses of proposed new rules. The interagency RARG was chaired by a member of the Council of Economic Advisors and was composed of members of executive branch economic and regulatory agencies and representatives from other agencies in the Executive Office of the President. CWPS provided staff support to RARG.

RARG focused its review on major rules, usually on about ten to twenty rules per year, that had an especially large impact (costing industry more than $100 million). It examined the rationale behind those regulations, the benefits they were intended to provide relative to the costs incurred, and their effectiveness in dealing with the problems they were meant to resolve. RARG reviews, when combined with preliminary economic analyses performed by CWPS, brought the economic impact of regulations under scrutiny at the level of the Executive Office of the President.   Through RARG reviews, President Carter hoped to establish "hegemony" over the largest regulatory actions of the regulatory agencies.

The participation of RARG in the regulatory review process was highly controversial. Interest groups that favored increased federal regulatory action questioned both (1) the propriety of RARG's participation after the regulatory agencies had completed their public comment period and (2) the extent of RARG's influence in regulation drafting.

A third area of controversy was the nature of reviews. Agency reviews were conducted largely by lawyers. Thus, the agency reviews emphasized design standards to achieve regulatory goals and were less than adequate at addressing economic issues. The RARG reviews were economic analyses conducted by economists. These types of studies tried to incorporate cost/benefit analyses and performance standards in the regulatory review process.

A fourth group (in addition to OIRA, CWPS, and RARG), the U.S. Regulatory Council, was established on October 31, 1978, to improve coordination of federal regulatory activities. This council was responsible for publishing a semiannual Calendar of Federal Regulations that listed all federal regulatory and rule-making activities in the *Federal Register*. (The regulatory calendar was discontinued by the Clinton administration.)

It was during this period that the legitimacy and timing of presidential review were first addressed by the courts, which were asked to decide whether it made a difference whether the president intervened before or after an agency's decision was made. These questions are addressed later in this chapter.

The Carter administration regulatory reform program had mixed results. Although OSHA eliminated over nine hundred minor safety rules (often referred to as "nuisance rules") in 1978, the overall burden of regulation on business continued to increase.

Reagan Administration

As part of its effort to promote private sector-led economic growth and reduce the role of government in the economy, regulatory policy was an important issue for the Reagan administration. The administration attempted to ensure that vital social and economic interests were considered during the regulatory review process—before regulations were promulgated and imple-mented. The result was a spate of executive orders, each with a very particular focus. Through this approach, regulatory review became increasingly narrow in its analysis of specific rules and potential impact areas. The policy focus at both the agency and OMB levels reflected this rule-specific, topic-specific orientation to regulatory review.

Within two weeks of taking office, President Reagan took several very visible actions on regulatory reform. He suspended hundreds of "midnight regulations" issued in the waning hours of the Carter administration, removed the price ceilings on domestic crude oil and gasoline, and abolished CWPS and its wage/price monitoring program.

Most of the early attention to regulation in the Reagan administration was directed by the Presidential Task Force on Regulatory Relief. Established by President Reagan in his first month in office and chaired by Vice President George Bush, this task force defined its mission as that of reforming the federal regulatory development and review system. The task force also prepared reviews of regulations in fourteen agencies, categorizing regulations as those to be approved, modified, withdrawn, or cancelled.

President Reagan also relied on a combination of executive orders and White House agencies to undertake regulatory reform. Less than one month into his first term, President Reagan signed EO 12291 ("Federal Regulation") which described a framework for improved economic analysis and oversight of regulations during the regulatory review process. The regulatory philosophy underlying the Reagan regulatory agenda was based on five principles:

- Administrative decisions should be taken with adequate information concerning the need for and consequences of the proposed government action:
- The potential benefits to society must outweigh the potential costs to society before regulatory action is undertaken;
- Regulatory objectives should maximize the net benefits to society;
- Of the several alternatives, the approach involving the least cost to society should be the one selected to achieve a regulatory objective;
- Agencies should set their regulatory priorities with the aim of maximizing the aggregate net benefits to society.

Building on President Carter's executive orders on regulation, EO 12291 included more specific requirements for economic analysis and balancing of costs and benefits. It required federal agencies to utilize cost/benefit analysis in all major rule making and to determine the most cost-effective approach for meeting any given regulatory objective.

Agencies were required to prepare an RIA to assess the costs and benefits of proposed rules estimated to have more than $100 million in net economic effects). These RIAs had to be submitted to OMB along with the proposed rules before they were published so that OMB could ensure that the agency was following the guidelines in EO 12291. Later, the agency was required to resubmit the revised rule to OMB after all the specified analyses had been performed but before the rule was made final. No major rule could be proposed or issued without OMB review and the cost/benefit analysis that accompanied it.

EO 12291 also set forth the outline of a process for regulatory review and oversight and identified analytical tools and techniques to be used at each stage of the regulatory decisionmaking process. The Reagan administration took the position that RARG had been an advisory agency to President Carter, whereas OMB would serve as the regulatory manager under President Reagan. OMB was charged with administering the executive orders, subject to the overall direction of the Presidential Task Force on Regulatory Relief. The greatest difference between RARG and Reagan's OMB was that RARG was involved *after* regulatory proposals were published in the *Federal Register*, and Reagan's OMB was involved *throughout* the regulatory process. Although OMB could not technically write or rewrite a regulation, knowledge that their rules would be reviewed required agencies to (1) be more aware of the costs and economic impacts of proposed rules, (2) be more careful in conducting their regulatory analyses, and (3) look for the lowest-cost means of implementing a regulation. Disagreements between OMB and the agencies were to be resolved by the Task Force. In its first year operating under EO 12291, OMB reviewed more than twenty-seven hundred regulations and regulatory proposals.

In June 1981, OMB issued guidelines for federal agencies to use in analyzing the impact of regulations. Called for in the guidelines were

- a statement of the need for and consequences of the proposed rule;
- an examination of alternative approaches to achieving the regulatory goals;
- an analysis of the expanded benefits and costs of the proposal, quantified to the greatest extent possible;
- an explanation of the reasons for choosing the proposed regulations rather than the alternatives;
- a statement of determination that the proposed regulatory action is within the agency's statutory responsibility.

To complement OIRA's regulatory authority, the office was also directed to enforce the Paperwork Reduction Act of 1990. OMB had to approve all federal forms and record-keeping requirements imposed on the public by the government to ensure that they were necessary and cost-effective.

The Task Force was disbanded in August 1983; the entire regulatory review program was then moved to OIRA. Although the regulatory reform efforts had some success in reducing the costs of regulation and in eliminating some regulations, they were criticized for not undertaking to rewrite the laws on which the regulations were based. Officials in OIRA were the targets of congressional criticism during the Reagan administration, as congressional oversight panels accused them of holding secret and restricted meetings. Such changes would have sped the pace of deregulation and ensured that the gains made in the regulatory reform program would not be undone in future years.

In January 1985, President Reagan issued EO 12498, which helped to refine the regulatory framework by requiring that all agencies submit proposed rules to OMB each year to ensure that they were consistent with the Reagan administration's regulatory policies. Federal agencies were required to describe their regulatory agendas, priorities, and proposed rules in an annual report, which was incorporated into a governmentwide regulatory program issued annually by OMB.

Other executive orders issued throughout the Reagan administration, such as EO 12606 and EO 12612 in 1987, further elaborated the review process by requiring explicit consideration of the potential effects of proposed regulations on family values and on federalism, respectively. Taken together, the many executive orders on regulation established a formal program of regulatory management.

Federal regulatory activity slowed for the most part during the Reagan years. The number of pages printed in the *Federal Register* fell steadily during the first six years of the Reagan administration from 63,554 pages in 1981 to 47,718 pages in 1986, the lowest number of pages since 1974. The number of pages rose slightly in 1987 and 1988.

Bush Administration

The regulatory review process was so time-consuming and cumbersome by the mid-1980s under the general terms of the Administrative Procedures Act (5 U.S.C. sec. 551–706) that various amendments to that law were passed in 1988. Two new measures, the Negotiated Rule Making Act and a companion bill dealing with regulatory dispute resolution, were passed in 1990.

Yet, many of the trends toward regulatory reform were reversed during the Bush administration. After unsuccessful efforts to appoint someone to serve as the administrator of OIRA, the Bush administration left the post vacant. Possibly as a consequence of essentially neglecting regulatory review by leaving the agency designated to perform it leaderless, the level and scope of federal regulation increased dramatically over the next three years.

With OIRA's lessened potency, the task of regulatory oversight was delegated in 1990 to the year-old Council on Competitiveness, chaired by Vice President Dan Quayle. The council's other members were the secretaries of the Treasury and Commerce, the attorney general, the chairman of the Council of Economic Advisors, and the president's chief of staff.

The council, with its small staff, was directed to (1) oversee the OMB review process to ensure that major new regulations did not place unnecessary burdens on businesses, (2) ensure that the benefits of rules outweighed the costs (i.e., that rules were cost-effective), and (3) mediate differences among executive branch agencies. The council claimed executive privilege for its contacts and communications. Its supporters regarded it as a necessary counter to the limited focus of agency rule making.

The council encountered a great deal of criticism during its tenure, as liberal lawmakers and public interest groups charged that it operated in secret and sought to weaken the rules developed by the regulatory agencies. Several House committees questioned the council's constitutionality and operations,[2] while some key congressmen attempted to curtail its activities by limiting and diverting its already meager resources.[3] Opponents viewed the council as an unofficial appeal mechanism for interests aggrieved by agency actions, or as a regulatory ombudsman superseding agency actions.

Some critics of the regulatory review process cited inadequacies in Executive Order 12291 itself and problems inherent in the ways in which certain methods and techniques are used in the regulatory review process. Agency analyses were perceived as self-serving by some critics of the process. Other critics claimed that OIRA reviews were a usurpation of congressional prerogatives.

In the January 1992 State of the Union Address, President Bush declared a ninety-day moratorium on new nonlegislatively mandated regulations as well as a reexamination of existing regulations in each federal agency. All agencies were directed to review regulations and programs that might hinder economic growth and to identify and accelerate action on initiatives that would reduce the burden of existing regulations or otherwise promote economic growth. As part of the review process, agencies had to ensure that the expected benefits to society of any new regulation should outweigh the expected costs it imposes on society.

Specific actions were also designated for those rules that addressed improving access to capital and improving the economic climate for small business. Rules that were in the regulatory process and those involving threats to health and safety were excluded from the moratorium. Bush also requested independent agencies to participate in the ninety-day moratorium. This presidential initiative was monitored by the Council on Competitiveness.

Various reasons have been offered to explain why the moratorium and review were undertaken. Some have maintained that two full years of regulatory budget increases, actual increases in the number and scope of regulations and in the number of staff in regulatory agencies, and a cover story in the November 30, 1991, issue of *National Journal* depicting President Bush as "The Regulatory President" (as well as similar articles in the press) may have spurred the White House to action. Others have suggested that the regulatory burden was out of control since OIRA had been without a permanent administrator since October 1989. President Bush's critics accused him of election year politicking. For his part, President Bush blamed the Congress for not enacting the administration's own regulatory reform proposals.

On April 2, 1992, Vice President Quayle held a press conference on the regulatory reform initiative and claimed that the ninety-day moratorium could produce savings of $10 to 20 billion annually. More than $2 billion of that savings came from the rules on union dues refunds that President Bush had announced earlier in the year. Over $1 billion was attributed to the accelerated approval of new drugs, with $1 to 3 billion realized by encouraging the use of more natural gas. More than $8 billion might stem from EPA rules changes.

President Bush extended the moratorium on new regulations for an additional 120 days on April 29, 1992, and asked the regulatory agencies to implement the regulatory reforms that they had identified during the original ninety-day moratorium. He then directed agency heads to report to him on September 1, 1992, on how they had implemented the changes, and to estimate the potential cost savings or other benefits to the economy created by the reforms.

Federal regulatory activity picked up again during the Bush administration. After a slight increase in 1989, the number of pages printed in the *Federal Register* decreased in 1990. However, the number of pages jumped 26 percent in 1991 to 67,716, around the time that Bush was being noted as "The Regulatory President."

Clinton Administration

The early regulatory actions of the Clinton administration painted a mixed picture. Deregulation was the order of the day for some sectors of the economy: financial services (for small business lending), communications (for auctioning licenses for radio waves), biotechnology (field testing of selected crops), and other sectors deemed essential for American competitiveness.

One area in which the Clinton administration appears to have improved upon the Bush administration is that it chose someone to head OMB's Office of Information and Regulatory Affairs. In addition, on September 20, 1993, Clinton issued EO 12866, which revoked EO 12291 and EO 12498, and established the administration's overall regulatory philosophy. EO 12866 directed agencies to "assess all costs and benefits of available regulatory alternatives including the alternative of not regulating." Costs and benefits are identified as both quantifiable and nonquantifiable measures. Vice President Gore directed an interagency project to create a White House system to review major regulatory proposals, and chairs an interagency group that sets the agenda for regulatory policy. EO 12866 is presented in Appendix B.

The Clinton administration has increased regulation dramatically, if one uses the number of pages in the *Federal Register* as a guide. The number of pages printed annually increased to 64,914 in 1994, compared to much lower numbers during most of the preceding twelve years. Among the areas seeing more aggressive regulatory action are environmental protection; prices, wages, services, and access in health care; workplace safety regulation; antitrust; affirmative action; and rules of compensation (i.e., minimum wage).

After three years in office, several conclusions can be reached about the Clinton administration's regulatory program. First, the issue of transparency remains. EO 12866 describes an institutional framework that allows the vice president to intervene in the regulatory process only at the request of an agency head or OIRA, not in response to a request from a private organization. Yet, EO 12866 does not require the vice president to disclose any conversations with OIRA, only formal intervention in a regulatory proceeding.

It was reported early in the administration that Vice President Gore or his aides were involved in regulatory decisions on Antarctica, biotechnology, and automobile fuel-efficiency standards, siding with environmentalists in those controversies. This is in sharp contrast to the recent past, when Congressman Gore was extremely critical of what he called OMB's "secret" collusion with business in the early years of the Reagan administration and Senator Gore was critical of the "secret" meetings of Quayle's Competitiveness Council.

A second issue relates to OIRA's level of participation in the regulatory process. Under Presidents Reagan and Bush, OMB had the authority to overrule regulatory agencies throughout the regulatory process; OMB found various points at which it could influence regulatory decision making. Under EO 12866, OIRA reviews only the most significant regulations, defined as those regulations that have an annual effect of $100 million on the economy (as determined by the agencies); create a serious inconsistency or interfere with the actions taken or planned by another regulatory agency; materially affect the budgetary impact of entitlements, grants, user fees, or loan programs; or raise novel legal or policy issues. Most decisions on the final form of regulation appear to be left to the regulatory agencies themselves.

A third issue is the success of EO 12866 after three years of operation. Disappointed with the progress that the regulatory agencies had made in the months following issuance of the executive order, President Clinton issued a regulatory reinvention initiative in 1995 that described plans for changing federal regulatory procedures because "not all agencies had taken the steps necessary to implement regulatory reform." Specific and separate reforms were announced for FDA, EPA, OSHA, pension rules, and the Medicare and Medicaid programs.

In January 1996, OMB issued new guidelines on the economic analysis of federal regulations to help regulatory agencies in the implementation of EO 12866. These guidelines, excerpted in Appendix C, supersede guidelines on preparing regulatory impact analyses that were issued in 1993. The major points raised in the new guidelines are: (1) economic analysis is a tool for regulatory decision makers, not an end or controlling factor; (2) efforts should be made to maximize the new benefits from regulation; and (3) the distributive effects, equity concerns, and qualitative benefits (nonquantifiable factors that cannot be verified or questioned with any degree of accuracy) associated with regulation should be emphasized in economic analysis.

A final issue that has arisen is that neither EO 12866 nor the new economic analysis guidelines do little to advance the concept of addressing employment impacts in regulatory decision making. For significant regulatory actions, agencies must assess the costs anticipated from regulatory actions, the direct cost to businesses in complying with the regulation, and any adverse effects on the efficient functioning of the economy and private markets (including productivity, employment, and competitiveness) together with a quantifying of those costs. Although EO 12866 and the guidelines expand the factors that can be considered in the analysis to include both quantifiable and qualitative measures, they do not target employment and wage effects as specific concerns to be addressed by regulators.

JUDICIAL REVIEW OF THE REGULATORY REVIEW PROCESS

In addition to administrative rules and procedures, the regulatory review process is the product of judicial review of agency actions. Although one might expect that judicial tests of the regulatory process and regulation had grown in both volume and scope over the years, such is not the case. Judicial action tends to be a lagging indicator of public policy concerns, since it is a lengthy procedure for cases to filter through the court system. As a result, only a few major cases touching on the regulatory review process have reached the Supreme Court. Nevertheless, when combined with congressional inquiries and other analyses, those cases address some of the key issues concerning the structure of the regulatory review process and the legally permissible approaches and techniques used in regulatory review.

The first of these cases addressed worker exposure to benzene, a toxic chemical used in gasoline and chemical manufacturing processes. In 1977, the National Institute for Occupational Safety and Health (NIOSH) concluded that benzene may cause leukemia and chromosome damage to workers exposed to the chemical. In response to the NIOSH study, OSHA issued an emergency temporary standard for workplace exposure to benzene in May 1977 and then promulgated a final exposure standard in February 1978.

The American Petroleum Institute (API) challenged the OSHA standard in the Fifth Circuit Court of Appeals on the grounds that compliance with the standard would be very costly, and that OSHA had not attempted to assess the benefits expected to be achieved by the standard. The Appeals Court ruled in API's favor. OSHA then requested the U.S. Department of Justice to petition the Supreme Court for a review of the Appeals Court decision.

In 1980, the case moved to the Supreme Court (*Industrial Union Department, AFL-CIO v. American Petroleum Institute*, 448 U.S. 607). The Supreme Court ruled that the OSHA standard to control worker exposure to benzene was invalid, and that OSHA had not met its burden of proving that the standards proposed were cost-beneficial. The Supreme Court had ruled in favor of cost/benefit analysis and directed OSHA that it must prove a significant risk to a worker's health before it imposed regulatory controls.

Despite the importance of the benzene case, a controversy over a workplace chemical that began years before the benzene case portended greater impact of presidential intervention and cost/benefit analysis. After a suit filed in 1975 by the Textile Workers Union of America, OSHA proposed in December 1976 to strengthen the national consensus standard for worker exposure to cotton dust at all stages of the textile manufacturing process; engineering controls would have to be installed and used to clean the air and reduce the level of exposure. It was claimed that cotton dust exposure led to a respiratory disease called byssinosis (commonly referred to as brown lung) that was extremely painful, debilitating, and, in some instances, fatal.

OSHA prepared an inflation impact statement on the proposed standard in compliance with President Ford's Executive Order 11821, which required that an economic analysis be performed for proposals that were expected to have a major impact on the economy. OSHA's analysis revealed that compliance with the proposed standard would cost the textile industry an estimated $2.7 billion in capital equipment costs and approximately $262 in annual operating costs. Approximately 390 cases of byssinosis would be prevented annually in yarn production and 1,360 cases prevented annually in weaving.

The proposed cotton dust standard and economic analysis underwent extensive review over the next eighteen months. Finally, in June 1977, CWPS released its review of the standard. CWPS concluded that although the basic assumptions underlying OSHA's economic analysis were correct, the benefits were overstated. CWPS also believed that (1) more flexibility was needed in the determination of the exposure standard and in the means for complying with the standard, and (2) OSHA's approach on those two issues was not the most technically or economically feasible means of reducing exposure to cotton dust.

OSHA responded in May 1978 by following some of CWPS's suggestions. Yet, OSHA was soon caught by surprise when President Carter's RARG announced that it was going to review the cotton dust rule. Although OSHA presented new information to RARG and CWPS later that month, RARG announced that it might request President Carter to order a delay in the issuance of the rule. This concerned OSHA as it had promised a federal court that the final cotton dust rule would be published by May 31, 1978.

On June 7, 1978, President Carter and Vice President Walter Mondale met with Secretary of Labor Ray Marshall, OSHA Administrator Eula Bingham, Council of Economic Advisors Chairman (and RARG Chairman) Charles Schultze, and Assistant to the President for Domestic Policy Stuart Eizenstat. (A 1978 review by the U.S. General Accounting Office determined that the ex parte contacts of CWPS, RARG, and President Carter were not illegal and would not, in any way, have invalidated the cotton dust rule.) A compromise was reached that would allow OSHA to issue a revised standard that would retain OSHA's provisions for engineering controls but would allow for variances to engineering controls if alternative approaches could achieve the same benefits.

Soon after the cotton dust rule was made final, the Amalgamated Clothing and Textile Workers Union and the American Textile Manufacturers Institute (ATMI) filed separate court challenges to the OSHA standard. The union argued that the rule failed to protect worker health. The association claimed the rule was highly inflationary and technologically unfeasible. After a series of legal maneuvers by the two sides, the case was heard by the D.C. Court of Appeals in February 1979. On February 24, 1979, the court rejected the industry arguments, claiming that OSHA had considered both the technical and economic issues during the regulatory process. ATMI said it would petition the U.S. Supreme Court for a hearing.

The "cotton dust" case highlighted the debate on the regulatory burden placed on business. This led Congress to provide some small measure of relief in 1980, before the case was heard by the Supreme Court. Two actions in particular by the Congress increased the president's role in regulatory review. First, Congress imposed regulatory analysis requirements for certain rule making actions in the Regulatory Flexibility Act of 1980. Then, the Congress required OMB clearances for the information-gathering efforts of executive branch agencies in the Paperwork Reduction Act of 1980.

The Supreme Court heard the arguments in the cotton dust case (*American Textile Manufacturers Institute et al. v. Donovan et al.*, 101 S. Ct. 2478) on January 21, 1981. ATMI reiterated its appeal court arguments and claimed that the same benefits to workers could be achieved through less costly approaches.

A third case involving the issue of presidential intervention in regulatory review arose in the courts in 1981 before the ruling on the cotton dust case. EPA had briefed President Carter and some White House staff, after the close of the public comment period, on the issues and options associated with an EPA ruling on new source performance standards governing the emission controls in coal burning power plants. In *Sierra Club v. Costle*, the Sierra Club questioned whether involvement of the president or his agents in the EPA regulatory proceeding was an ex parte contact that "tainted" the regulatory process. On April 29, 1981, the Court of Appeals for the District of Columbia rejected the challenge. The court ruled that key executive branch policymakers could not be isolated from each other or from the president, and recognized the need for the president and White House staff to monitor the consistency of executive branch agency regulations with administration policy. The court's upholding the concept of "intraexecutive contacts" between a president's staff and agency staff helped to buttress the arguments being made by the new Reagan administration for a strong role for OMB in regulatory review.

Before the Supreme Court announced its decision in the cotton dust case, the Reagan White House intervened in the cotton dust regulatory process. Fearing that the Supreme Court's decision would impede President Reagan's effort to free business from the burden of government regulation, the administration asked the court in March 1981 to vacate the February 1979 Court of Appeals opinion and send the standard back to OSHA for further consideration. The administration indicated its desire to impose a cost/benefit test on the cotton dust standard and explore the overall usefulness of cost/benefit analysis in setting worker health standards.

The Supreme Court rejected the administration's request to vacate the Court of Appeals decision. The court was, in effect, warning the administration that the newly issued Executive Order 12291 and its requirements for cost/benefit analysis could not take the place of having the administration request Congress to amend the Occupational Safety and Health Act to require cost/benefit analysis. The decision might have been a precursor to the court's soon-to-be-announced decision on the cotton dust case.

Finally, on June 17, 1981, one year after its ruling in the "benzene" case, the Supreme Court upheld OSHA's cotton dust standard, declaring that a cost/benefit analysis was unnecessary. As in the "benzene" case, Congress's delegation of authority to OSHA to set such standards was reaffirmed. The Supreme Court ruled that the Occupational Safety and Health Act did not require OSHA to determine whether the costs of the cotton dust standard bore a reasonable relationship to its benefits, nor, for that matter, was such an analysis necessary when promulgating any health standard. The issue of cost was not part of the act; the Court noted that Congress had included requirements for cost/benefit analyses in other laws but not this one.

The court did not address the issue of whether cost/benefit analysis might be required for rules issued under other parts of the act, such as safety regulations. In addition, the court did not address the issue of whether presidential involvement in the cotton dust rule-making process was legal.

Although the Reagan administration's regulatory reform efforts were temporarily slowed by the Supreme Court's decision in the cotton dust case, the administration did try to interpret the ruling in such a way as to justify institutionalizing cost/benefit analysis in agency rule-making procedures. The administration claimed that the court's decision affected only selected provisions of the Occupational Safety and Health Act, and that it, in effect, strengthened the mandate of other laws that required the use of cost/benefit analysis.

At about the time that the Supreme Court was handing down its decision in the cotton dust case, President Reagan's desire to incorporate cost/benefit analysis into agency rule making was criticized in a 1981 Congressional Research Service (CRS) report that considered the procedures outlined under Executive Order 12291 to be an intrusion of the institutional safeguards for administrative process as delineated by the Administrative Procedure Act (U.S. House of Representatives 1981a). That CRS study also claimed that the Reagan administration's regulatory review program went beyond the Sierra Club decision. The CRS study said that Executive Order 12291:

> conflicted with APA procedures for flexibility by establishing a central coordinating agency for the process of informal rule making, and by vesting it with the authority to create and enforce substantively oriented procedures designed to direct and control that process;

- displaced the discretionary authority of agency decisionmakers in violation of congressional delegations of rule-making authority because of the OMB director's enforcement authority;
- created a critical access point to the agency decisionmaking process without providing safeguards against secret, undisclosed, and unreviewable contacts by government and nongovernment interests seeking to influence the agency.

The Reagan administration disagreed with the CRS study which, of course, had no force of law.

Agency rule making was further strengthened in the Supreme Court's 1984 Chevron decision (*Chevron U.S.A., Inc. v. National Resources Defense Council,* 467 U.S. 837 (1984)). This case set forth the doctrine that if Congress has not clearly stated its wishes regarding a regulation and the agency has met all procedural tests in formulating its regulations, courts are to give deference to agency decisions.

The Supreme Court's current docket has few regulatory cases before it. However, the lower courts are likely to be making further rulings on the permissible scope and bases of agency rule making throughout the next decade because (1) many more cases involving EPA and OSHA regulations, and regulations implementing the Americans with Disabilities Act, are producing a greater volume of litigation; and (2) the tactic of challenging the *process* of developing a regulation, in addition to (or instead of) merely the *substance* of a regulation, is becoming more widespread.

These court decisions and administrative reviews lead one to conclude that presidential intervention *in* the regulatory process is permissible under certain circumstances, but that intervention *with* the process is not permissible.

CONCLUSION

None of the recent White House occupants or staff has addressed structural change in the regulatory process. Few efforts have been made to amend legislation as a way of institutionalizing and making more permanent changes in the techniques or parameters of regulatory analysis. Although the federal policy context for regulatory reform may appear daunting and not nearly so malleable as new arrivals to the federal policy process may believe, it is still feasible to incorporate assessment of such factors as employment and wage effects of regulation into the regulatory process. The scope of any presidential executive order on regulation needs to be broadened to include independent regulatory agencies if systemwide reform is to take place, one of the many recommendations presented addressed in the next chapter.

NOTES

1. The president's authority to exercise oversight over the regulatory process was based initially on his constitutional power to "take care that the laws be faithfully executed" (Article II, Section 3). This authority over executive branch agencies was reaffirmed in *Myers v. United States* (1926) and *Youngstown Sheet & Tube Co. v. Sawyer* (1952). The president's authority over "independent" agencies has always been more problematical. *Humphrey's Executor v. United States* (1935) limited the president's authority in this area to making nominations and to removing for "cause." In recent years, independent agencies have cooperated somewhat with the president in implementing executive orders. In passing the Paperwork Reduction Act (P.L. 96–511), Congress gave the Office of Management and Budget (OMB) a direct role in coordinating agency regulations that imposed an increased paperwork burden on the public, including those of independent regulatory agencies. Regulatory agencies were allowed to override an OMB decision, but that law did initiate a move to extend executive branch control over the independent agencies.

2. See, e.g., U.S. General Accounting Office, *Risk-Risk Analysis: OMB's Review of a Proposed OSHA Rule* (Washington, D.C.: U.S. Government Printing Office, July 1992) (GAO/PEMD-92-33).

3. See, e.g., Philip J. Hilts, "Quayle Council Debate: Issue of Control," *The New York Times*, December 16, 1991, p. B11.

Approaches for Reform: Addressing Employment Effects in Regulatory Decision Making

Three major conclusions may be drawn about the regulatory decision-making process from the preceding analysis:

- Neither short-term employment effects nor changes in employment patterns over time can be adequately addressed by the methods currently used in the regulatory development process.
- Regulatory agencies and the contractors who work for them performing regulatory analyses have little incentive to develop new methods or techniques, or to expand those they are currently using to incorporate additional factors or different assumptions and data bases.
- Recent presidential administrations have not addressed structural change in the regulatory process. Few, if any, efforts have been made to amend legislation to make permanent changes in the techniques or parameters of regulatory analysis.

Upon the basis of those conclusions, this chapter presents recommendations to improve the regulatory analysis and review procedures in general and to account for employment effects in regulatory analysis in particular. The recommendations revolve around three concepts:

- A new policy framework for regulation is needed to redirect the regulatory decision-making process so that the process is more responsive to the needs of economic growth, the private sector, and to the employment effects of regulation.
- Improved oversight and coordination (by Congress and the White House) are needed in the regulatory decisionmaking process to ensure that the economywide impacts of regulations on employment patterns and wage levels are considered in promulgating regulations.
- Regulatory analysts need to use state-of-the-art analytical tools in order so they can better determine the employment effects of their regulatory actions.

DEVELOPING A POLICY FRAMEWORK FOR REGULATION

Economic growth is the first best solution to increasing employment. We have come to expect that government at all levels—federal, state, and local—will pursue policies and programs that enhance opportunities for economic growth and employment: policies that look out for the future American work force, that do not extinguish the flame of hope. Many believe that government regulations should impose the lowest possible burden on the economy. In other words, the government should follow the well-known prescription: Do no harm.

Consequently, the nation's workers should not find themselves put out of work by the actions of their own government. It is difficult enough when workers lose their jobs because of changes in competition, imports, or technology. Government should get out of the way and let entrepreneurs—in big and small businesses alike—create the jobs, create the growth.

As our experiences with the spotted owl, the luxury tax, and countless other rules are now telling us, government should not take any actions that deliberately and unnecessarily result in worker dislocations and layoffs. How the average worker will be affected by a regulation should be among the first things considered by a regulator. Yet rarely are the employment impacts of regulations addressed in the regulatory development process. How often do regulators consider reductions in the number of new employees hired, the dismissal of current employees, and the reductions in salaries or wages (where such flexibility exists)? Not often enough.

Initially, a new framework is needed for the government regulation of economic activity. Three points need to be made as we enter the twenty-first century—about the legislative and executive branches and the regulatory agencies themselves. For more than twenty-five years, the Congress's role in regulation has been to pass fairly broad-based laws that provided executive branch and independent agency regulators with a great deal of latitude in promulgating regulations. Oversight hearings focused mostly on why the pace and depth of regulation weren't faster and deeper, and on the methods that the White House (both Democratic and Republican) used to oversee the regulatory process.

We are now faced with a different type of situation. The 1994 elections changed a great many perceptions about what can and cannot be accomplished in government and politics. Oversight hearings now focus on the excesses of the past twenty-five years, and on the burdens that regulation imposes on business—and its accompanying cost in terms of jobs, competitiveness, productivity, and economic growth.

Congress needs to exercise vigorously its oversight function over regulatory agencies to ensure that the regulations promulgated by those agencies stay true to their legislative mandate and do not go beyond the intent of Congress.

Congress also needs to legislate more precisely. Many hearings are held and many experts are heard from. There are hundreds of congressional staffers available to write laws. Congress needs to give more guidance and less leeway to regulators.

With respect to the executive branch, one lesson of the past twenty-five years is that people is policy (of course, not a lesson that should be lost on members of Congress when they hire staff as well). Some of the most prescient advances in regulatory policy and deregulation were made by having the right people at OMB or at the head of some regulatory agencies. In contrast, even the agenda of the Reagan administration suffered as some appointees were less than committed to deregulation and the power of the marketplace.

As the natural tendency of the bureaucracy is to lean toward more regulation and slow reform of existing rules, presidents need to appoint committed deregulators. Those appointees must be willing to take on the bureaucracy and the special interests in order to make the regulatory process more open, more fair, and more reasonable.

The regulatory agencies are not without blame in this period of regulatory overkill. Three steps are needed to curb regulatory excess.

First, the regulatory process should focus on implementation of the true intent of laws and not on frivolous or technical rules. By punishing companies for violations relating to paperwork, filings, postings, and procedures, regulators are focusing on the small picture and missing the larger issue associated with government regulation of the workplace and the economy. Is the posting of a sign in a three-person work site really relevant if the work site is safe and all three employees follow appropriate procedures? Is the absence of that sign worth thousands of dollars in fines? More and more often, it seems that the technical rules are being used to push broad social and political agendas that have little to do with the original intent of the regulation or its organic legislation.

Second, regulatory agencies need to develop internal procedures to ensure that the regulations that they promulgate stay within the bounds of their legislative mandates, thereby preventing excessive adverse impacts on employment levels and wages. Each regulatory agency or cabinet department should consider setting up a central regulatory review office that will serve in an adversarial role to the regulation promulgators—an office that will question the need for and costs associated with regulation before the regulation is sent to the Office of Management and Budget.

Finally, regulations should be drafted in a way that explicitly considers their employment effects. More appropriate and comprehensive methods and models are needed by regulatory agencies to address the employment effects of regulation and assess the costs and benefits of regulatory actions in regulatory analyses. Regulators need to be concerned about the employment effects of regulations on both the particular sector being regulated and on other sectors that might interact with, or be affected by, the regulated sector.

IMPROVING REGULATORY OVERSIGHT, MANAGEMENT, AND REVIEW

Four major approaches are presented here to modify the federal regulatory process in order to develop a systematic consideration of the overall effects of regulation on the U.S. economy as a whole, and of employment effects in particular.

Strengthen Regulatory Review in the White House

Any presidential executive order on regulation should state clearly OMB's authority to set standards for regulatory review and to monitor agency compliance. Executive Order 12291 contained broad review authority for OMB. Executive Order 12866 narrows that authority. The former approach is preferred. OMB's authority over regulatory review and the regulatory development process should be broadened from the review of individual rules to the larger issues posed by an agency's entire regulatory program, and OMB should be given greater authority to monitor and enforce agency practices during the regulatory process. EO 12866 should be amended to ensure that OMB can expand its functions beyond the technical review function of determining whether regulatory analyses have been done, and allow OMB to set aggressive standards for considering economic and employment effects in regulatory analyses, evaluate the agencies' processes and results, and coordinate regulatory actions among agencies.

Extend the Coverage of Presidential Executive Orders on Regulation to Independent Regulatory Agencies

An obstacle to the development of a coherent regulatory framework is that the vast majority of rules and regulations are either explicitly exempt from, or for other reasons not subject to, the executive orders covering regulatory review. For example, regulations taking the form of procedural rules, such as those specifying the steps for applying for government-sponsored grants, contracts, certifications, or other benefits are not generally considered to be regulations that impose costs upon citizens, organizations, or the economy. In fact, of course, such rules do impose paperwork burdens, introduce delays, and sometimes result in significant hardship to individuals and organizations, which ultimately affects the economy.

There are also exemptions for certain agencies. OMB has interpreted EO 12866 as applying to independent agencies only in relation to the review process of regulatory planning and coordination. A great deal of the economic regulation of business remains intact and outside the executive branch and the direct oversight of the president. As noted earlier, most economic regulation is implemented by agencies that are statutorily independent of the executive branch whereas most social regulation is conducted by agencies within the executive branch.

Executive branch oversight over the regulatory process should be extended to the independent regulatory agencies. The scope of the current executive order on regulation should be broadened to require that independent regulatory agencies be held to a strong standard of external (i.e., White House-level) review. Such coverage is the result of a natural progression in government accountability, the increased coverage of executive branch oversight over the independent agencies as demonstrated by legislative mandates such as the Government in the Sunshine Act of 1976, and the willingness of independent agency heads to cooperate with the executive orders issued by Presidents Reagan and Bush.

Regarding the issue of transparency, the regulatory agencies and OMB are already covered by the Freedom of Information Act and the "Sunshine Act." Therefore, a revised regulatory review structure would not seem to require any additional rules in order to ensure public accountability. There are so many different and diverse ways for citizens and interested groups to be participants in the policy process that it is difficult to accept the notion that regulatory review is a closed process. The norms of openness and technical soundness in regulatory review are not incompatible; in fact, the prospect of public scrutiny actually should encourage sound analysis using methods rigorous enough to withstand such scrutiny. However, adding reporting and record-keeping requirements for review agencies—as advocated by some in Congress—would only divert review bodies from their basic functions.

Regulatory Budget

A third approach to rectifying perceived problems with the U.S. regulatory regime is the regulatory budget. Quite simply, a regulatory budget would be the equivalent of a financial budget for each government agency. Instead of an allocation of dollars to be spent by the agency in pursuit of its programs and legislative mandates, each agency would receive a regulation impact allocation, which it could "spend" during a given period.

Supporters of such an approach argue that a regulatory budget would instill a measure of discipline into the regulatory programs of agencies, by compelling agencies whose regulations have far-reaching and significant impacts on the economy to make decisions at the agency level that involve sensitive trade-offs between regulatory interests.[1] Proponents of regulatory budgeting further contend that a regulatory budget will constrain the growth of regulation and make it more cost-beneficial for society. The Brookings Institution as well as the Joint Economic Committee of the U.S. Congress have at various times espoused this approach, and it has some support within OMB.

A regulatory agency's tendency to lower its estimates of the economic and employment impacts of proposed regulatory actions artificially (as the agency determined how to "spend" its regulatory allocation) would be countered or mitigated by the use of computable general equilibrium models (noted in the following pages), accompanied by transparent assumptions and data. Critics of the regulatory budget concept maintain that agencies may not undertake the rigorous analyses necessary to support difficult decisions among those regulatory initiatives over which they have discretion.[2]

A variety of factors involving time, money, and personnel can act as impediments to an agency's undertaking such analyses. Also, critics of regulatory budgeting argue that it interjects agency rule making into even more tangled political processes where the alleged advantages of the regulatory budget can be more easily undermined. This could occur, for example, at the "front end" of the process, when regulatory budget allocations to an agency are being determined, as is currently the case with fiscal budgeting. Deviations from the regulatory budget could also occur after the fact by appeals to Congress, special interests, or even the White House. Overall, the regulatory budget concept, although admirable in principle, presents many challenges that limit it as a vehicle for better addressing employment effects of regulation.

Negotiated Rule Making

The use of negotiated rule making may improve the regulatory process to take account of potentially negative economic impacts. In negotiated rule making, the parties likely to be affected by the regulation, and any others interested in the subject under consideration, meet with agency regulators and, in effect, negotiate the regulation. The regulatory review process for the negotiated rule then proceeds as stipulated in the Administrative Procedure Act and the elaborating executive orders, agency rules, and other relevant legislation.

The most frequent uses of "neg-reg" (as it is called) have been applied to regulations from the Departments of Commerce and Interior that clearly affect specific industries (such as the Commerce Department's regulations on the tuna fishing industry). This technique will likely continue to be used for regulations affecting specific industries, as it tends to make the regulatory process less adversarial and ensure that particular industry processes and operating factors are considered in crafting the regulation.

President Clinton addressed the issue of negotiated rule making in a September 30, 1993, memorandum. The President directed the regulatory agencies to explore and, where appropriate, use "consensual mechanisms" for developing regulations, including negotiated rule making.

Yet, using this technique would add little to broad assessments of employment effects. Specific industry employment effects could be considered only to the extent that employers affected by the proposed regulation were parties to the negotiation of the rule and were able to determine the likely employment and wage effects on their company or industry. Even the most vigorous proponents of "neg-reg," such as the Administrative Conference of the United States, admit that it is not suitable for many regulatory situations, and certainly not for broad-scale regulations from EPA and OSHA with economywide impacts (Pritzker 1992).

In terms of addressing employment effects, the same criticisms that pertain to cost/benefit techniques in general would still apply if a full-scale impact analysis is required and if conventional cost/benefit techniques are used in the regulatory development stage. However, negotiated regulation may be a satisfactory approach in the regulatory process for assessing employment effects in sectors directly affected by the regulation when a regulation is not of sufficient scope—or its impacts would not be of sufficient magnitude—to warrant a full-scale regulatory review.

IMPROVING REGULATORY ANALYSIS

Although there are numerous ways to improve regulatory analysis, two approaches in particular would result in broadening the policy focus in, and changing the analytical tools for, regulatory review: (1) refinements in techniques for assessing the costs and benefits of proposed and existing regulations (such as risk-risk and health-health analysis) and (2) the use of macroanalysis tools and techniques. These two approaches are examined in light of their relevance and potential for addressing employment effects in the regulatory development process. The discussion of those two approaches is followed by recommendations on how improved analytical techniques could be integrated into the current regulatory development process.

Refining Cost/Benefit Assessment Techniques

A number of refinements to the methods of calculating the costs and benefits of regulation have been introduced into the federal regulatory decision-making process over the past decade. The process has become more technical and, correspondingly, individuals associated with the process are more technically sophisticated and knowledgeable about the use of conventional economic analysis tools such as cost/benefit analysis. In addition, after President Reagan's Executive Order 12291 required cost/benefit analysis for many major regulations (those with estimated costs of more than $100 million), use of these techniques became increasingly common—if not by all agency staffs, at least by the outside contractors who prepare the required regulatory analyses.

OMB staff, as well as scholars in academic and policy research institutions who follow regulatory policy, have also suggested refinements in the cost/benefit approach to assessing regulatory impacts. Within the past several years, for example, various proposals have been made by OMB, the Institute for Regulatory Reform, Citizens for a Sound Economy, the Heritage Foundation, and the American Enterprise Institute, among others, for undertaking rigorous "risk assessments" *before* a health-and-safety regulation is even proposed. This would allow the magnitude of the health, safety, or environmental risks that are to be mitigated by a regulation to be weighed against the estimated costs of imposing the regulation. These proposals have been controversial; GAO criticized OMB's review of a proposed OSHA rule using "risk-risk" analysis as illegal under the Supreme Court's cotton dust ruling.[3] Nevertheless, these risk assessments (and a twenty-three step review process) have become the cornerstone of the regulatory reform initiative (The Job Creation and Wage Enhancement Act) passed by the House of Representatives under the Contract with America.

Most recently, what has been termed "health-health" analysis has been described as a better method to evaluate health-and-safety regulation. This approach is based on the relationship between wealth and health. Wealth refers to an individual's command over goods and services; health measures the annual risk of death and overall life expectancy. Instead of focusing on the costs and benefits (expressed in dollars) of regulations that are intended to reduce health risks, it measures trade offs between numbers of lives saved with and without a proposed regulation. It contrasts funds directed at regulatory compliance with funds used for nonregulatory purposes and analyzes the choices made by people.

Those refinements are based on a costs-versus-benefits approach, in which costs and benefits are measured in terms of lives or person-years saved rather than dollars. None of them measures costs or benefits in terms of jobs. These measures are unlikely to assist in addressing the broad employment effects of regulation to the extent that they (1) are measured in terms other than jobs, (2) involve studying only one rule or regulation at a time, and (3) do not capture indirect and spillover effects as a regulation's effects filter through the economy. Nevertheless, those refinements do improve the regulatory development process.

Using Macro-Analysis Tools

A most promising technical improvement to the regulatory development process, in terms of better addressing employment effects, is the use of broad-gauge, economywide analytical tools and techniques. The development of better, more rigorous, and comprehensive economic and computer models and methods for addressing the effects of regulation would greatly increase the general understanding of the effects of regulation on wage and employment levels. This approach would also substantially enhance the ability of federal regulatory agencies to address employment effects properly, and to take them fully into consideration in the rule making and regulatory enforcement processes.

Such methods and models should include (but not necessarily be limited to) a framework based on a generalized model of the economy. One possible approach that may be used involves the "general equilibrium" models and methods that have already been developed for the purpose of evaluating tax policies (see Chapters 3 and 4). These computational or computable general equilibrium (CGE) models could be adapted to conduct the explicit analysis of regulation and, with further modifications, the effects of regulation both on employment and on overall economic activity.

The most important feature of a CGE model is its incorporation of the interaction of sectors and of spillover effects from one sector to another in the economy. It permits taking into account interactions throughout the economy in a consistent and systematic manner. All sectors are linked, not only through the labor market, but also through the other markets in which firms buy and sell goods for use as inputs into their own production processes. It is important to include these linkages when evaluating employment effects. If one part of the economy is changed as a result of a new regulation, then there will be effects on the other parts of the economy. Excluding those changes would greatly underestimate the employment impact of the regulatory process.

A CGE model also allows for substitution, both in production and in consumption. In producing goods, employers respond to changing costs (such as might result from new regulation) by adjusting the technology that they use; new technologies may be more or less labor intensive (although historically they have typically been less labor-intensive). Similarly, consumers adjust their consumption of different goods after changes in prices due to regulatory changes. An analysis that does not take these substitution possibilities into consideration can misjudge the magnitude as well as the direction of change in employment.

Adopting a CGE model for estimating employment effects in the regulatory development process is a sophisticated technical step. The general model needs to be designed to meet the specific needs of the user. Some of these tailoring requirements, such as distinguishing among workers by particular occupations or industries, is done fairly easily. Other requirements (such as modeling structural unemployment, union behavior, or industry wage differentials) involve much more precise and detailed work in terms of resolving a number of theoretical and empirical issues.

Finally, it is important to recognize the transparency of these models in terms of the ability of the model users to explain results that, at first, seem counterintuitive. The successful use of CGE models is enhanced if regulatory decision makers, career civil servants, contractors, and the private sector work together to ensure the integrity of the model, its assumptions and inputs, and its results. The participants need first to decide carefully on how the regulatory policy is to be modeled. This is especially important when collecting data on the changes in the affected sectors or parts of the economy.

Equally important is agreement on the procedures for deciphering and interpreting the detailed output that results; the workings of the CGE model should be transparent to the model users (who would require training for this purpose) to explain results. Given that the models are based on consistent and well-accepted behavioral theories in economics, any economist trained to work with CGE models should be able to explain each result.

Integrating Broader Analytical Tools into the Regulatory Development Process

Improvements in regulatory analysis procedures could be effected through legislation or amendments to presidential executive orders on regulation. Of course, executive orders can be enacted more rapidly than legislation and preserve their drafters' intent without having to be negotiated through a legislative bargaining process.

President Reagan's EO 12291 provided a framework within which the employment effects of existing and proposed regulations could be addressed, identifying "significant adverse effects on employment" as one of the elements constituting a "major rule" for which a formal regulatory impact analysis is required. Executive Order 12866 does not contain such a framework.

Regulatory agencies should be required to address employment and wage effects explicitly in the regulatory review process. President Clinton should amend EO 12866 or the economic analysis guidelines issued on January 11, 1996, to implement EO 12866 to include provisions that require the agencies to develop and utilize CGE models at some stage of the regulatory review process. The amendment should include minimum requirements and timetables for incorporating CGE models into agencies' existing processes and procedures so that they may assess economywide impacts on factors such as employment and wages, and capture the cumulative effects of the agency's past and proposed regulatory actions.

With these changes, a regulatory agency would continue to perform initial regulatory review using both cost/benefit techniques and, whenever indicated, broader-gauged techniques (such as CGE models) to assess employment impacts of a particular regulation throughout the economy as well as the cumulative employment effects of all the agency's regulations. Agencies would be directed to broaden the focus of their review and consider each proposed new regulation in light of their overall regulatory programs, including already existing regulations and all other proposed regulations.

Since the resources available to the regulatory agencies are often limited and bureaucracies are slow to adopt innovative techniques, some agencies might react negatively to a requirement that they utilize a CGE model. Therefore, the more precisely written the executive order, the more likely it is that its provisions will be carried out. In addition, Congress should consider appropriating funds for regulatory agencies to develop and utilize CGE models. Although the up-front costs may appear high, the return on Congress's investment will be a more honest and more transparent analysis of regulatory costs and impacts on the economy and on employment.

On the other hand, legislation would be an ideal way to codify new regulatory procedures that would be uniform among agencies. Of course, passing legislation is time-consuming and a bill may find its intent and content are highly likely to be modified—if not distorted—as it passes through the various committees and chambers of the legislature. However, once passed, this type of legislation would be difficult to amend (and, unlike an executive order, not reversible with a change in the presidency).

CONCLUSION

Bold action needs to be taken by both the president and the Congress in order to improve the way the government regulates the workplace and the economy. With the exception of the fact that it has rarely happened over the past twenty-five years, it should go without saying that the president and the Congress must work together to assure a regulatory decision-making process that addresses the employment effects of regulations and accounts for economywide issues. The regulatory decision-making process should also be made more credible, transparent, and technically sound.

NOTES

1. See, e.g., John F. Morrall III, "Controlling Regulatory Costs: The Use of Regulatory Budgeting," a paper prepared for the Public Management Service of the Organization for Economic Cooperation and Development, Paris, July 1992.

2. Such views were expressed, for example, by some of the panelists at a symposium on regulatory budgeting sponsored by the American Bar Association's Administrative Law and Regulatory Practice Section in Washington, D.C., October 2, 1992.

3. U.S. General Accounting Office, *Risk–Risk Analysis: OMB's Review of a Proposed OSHA Rule* (Washington, D.C.: U.S. Government Printing Office, July 1992) (GAO/PEMD-92-33).

Appendix A
Estimating Employment Effects Using Computational General Equilibrium Models

Government regulation of economic and social activity in the United States affects employment in ways that are often very complicated. Regulation of one industry or activity may have both expected and unexpected spillover effects on other industries or activities. This spillover follows from the interdependent nature of most economic activity: one sector's demand is another's supply. An analysis of the employment effects of regulatory policy suggests that attention be paid to how regulatory policy affects both overall economic activity and labor markets. For this reason, it is natural to look to computable general equilibrium (CGE) models as an instrument for estimating the employment effects of government regulations because they incorporate such spillover effects in a direct and obvious way.

COMPUTABLE GENERAL EQUILIBRIUM MODELS

There are many choices that must be made in developing a model to address employment effects in the regulatory process. The results that emerge from any model depend on the assumptions that underlie it. This problem is particularly severe in large-scale CGE models. The risk, then, is that the model is not transparent in the sense of explaining apparently counterintuitive results that might emerge. A problem arises if inappropriate modeling assumptions are applied. To remedy this, the policymaker using the results of a CGE simulation must be aware of the broad choices that are available. This appendix briefly addresses some of the major questions that should be asked in any policy application of CGE models.

Why Use a CGE Model?

The principal advantage of using a CGE model in assessing the employment effects of regulation is that it permits taking into account interactions throughout the economy in a consistent manner. If something is changed in one part of the economy as a result of regulation, then there will be effects on the other parts of the economy, and these are automatically taken into account when one computes effects by using a general equilibrium model.

"Computational" or "computable" general equilibrium or CGE models are natural extensions of older input-output models, which have been widely used for decades to measure the effects of public policies. But CGE models are vastly more sophisticated, in large part as a result of technological developments in computer software and the ability of modelers to manage huge data bases, as well as enhanced understanding of the underlying economic processes being modeled. CGE models usually require extremely large amounts of data and the application of even more sophisticated statistical techniques than the methods described in Chapter 4. These models traditionally have required relatively powerful computers and large amounts of computing time because of their intricacy and complexity; however, computer facilities and running time have become less of a constraint on the use of these general equilibrium models as the processing speed and memory capacity of computers have increased.

CGE models extend the input-output models to take into account substitution possibilities in terms of, for example, labor- or capital-intensive technology choices as well as the circular flow of income across consuming households and producing firms generated by policies such as regulation. Although it is possible to make *ad hoc* extensions of input-output models to incorporate some of these concerns, that approach is effectively constructing a CGE model indirectly. Thus, a CGE model provides a straightforward approach that builds on earlier models used for policy impact analysis.

Another important reason for using a CGE model, or indeed any multisectoral model, in addressing employment effects is that it provides comparative results for a range of employment sectors. Many regulations are reviewed by agencies concerned only about the particular sector being regulated (such as the Federal Communications Commission and the radio industry). The issue then is whether any decisionmaker is concerned with the overall, economywide impacts on employment of the regulations in particular sectors. In the absence of some type of multisectoral model being used to assess these impacts, the likelihood is that they will not be quantified.

Because so much recent health, safety, environmental, and civil rights regulation in the United States applies to all employment sectors, using economywide models to assess employment effects is essential. Even if regulation appears to be sectoral in the sense of only applying to one or a few sectors, there will likely be important employment effects in other sectors due to the interactive nature of the economy.

How a CGE Model Works

A CGE model works by using data to describe the economy in a benchmark year, and by then varying one or more elements so as to "shock" the economy and change the values of data items. Finally, the model then compares the new and original values for the economy as a whole and for each component.

A CGE model can be shocked by changing a policy such as imposing a regulation that sets requirements that alter resource allocation. The model can then be solved for a new general equilibrium, and the results compared to the original equilibrium. A good deal of early research in CGE models was directed at just being able to solve them, since that is not a trivial computational task. Recent developments have relieved modelers of those concerns, and attention is now more properly turning to the specification and use of CGE models in policy analysis. CGE models are eminently suited to assessing the employment effects of regulation because of their broad, economywide scope and ability to handle large amounts of data and many variables.

Results that are generated with a CGE model may be contrasted with approaches that have been used previously in regulatory impact analyses (RIAs). In general, those approaches failed to take into account the economy-wide implications of regulatory policy changes, and focused on the employment impact in a handful of sectors that were presumed to be the ones most directly affected by the change. If some regulatory policy was expected to reduce the demand for low-sulfur coal, for example, then employment impacts on the coal industry were estimated. No impacts on employment in sectors that *used* coal as an input were studied, as would be the case when using a CGE model.

The other general problem with existing approaches to conducting an RIA is the absence of any allowance for the substitutability of labor for other factors of production. If the price of labor increases, then economic theory suggests that a profit-maximizing firm will look for ways to use more capital-intensive techniques. This change in technology is not at all implausible. It might take the form of simply replacing several secretaries on typewriters with an efficient word processor, or several clerks with a computer-automated billing system.

Studies by Hazilla and Kopp (1990), Jorgenson and Slesnick (1985), and Jorgenson and Wilcoxen (1990a) (1990b) use CGE models to study the effects of regulations. Although the focus of these studies was on the welfare and equity effects of regulations, the underlying CGE models would have captured employment effects with some sectoral detail. CGE models have been used to study the effects of domestic environmental policy by Ballard and Medema (1989), Bergman (1991), Boyd and Uri (1991), Hazilla and Kopp (1990), Johnson (1980), Jorgenson and Wilcoxen (1990a) (1990b), and Nestor and Pasurka (1992a) (1992b).

A CGE model allows for such variations in substitutability as sectors differ in their ability to substitute labor for other factors. For example, service sectors tend to have a high degree of substitutability compared to manufacturing or mining sectors. These differences can be important for employment impacts of regulations to the extent that regulations impact sectors differently.

What a CGE Model Looks Like

A CGE model is basically a large set of demand and supply functions that cover every market, for both commodities and factors of production in the economy. The demand side of commodity markets comprises private households, government agents, and firms. Some of these agents are domestic, and some are foreign and therefore capture export demand. Private households are able to buy only as much as their income allows them. They receive this income as they sell labor services to firms, but they also receive a return on any capital investment that they have made. In the model, all private households are aggregated into one representative household that captures the aggregate expenditure pattern in the economy.

As private households sell their labor and capital services to firms, this enables firms to produce. In addition to buying these primary production factors, firms also buy intermediate inputs from each other. Commodity purchases by all agents comprise both imported and domestically produced goods.

In addition to participating in the regulatory process, the government has a number of tax and subsidy instruments available for redistributive uses. Income and sales taxes, as well as import tariffs, are all included in this illustrative model. If a subsidy is needed in a regulatory process, some or all of these taxes can be adjusted automatically to incorporate the additional employment effects that the funding of this subsidy will cause.

There are important opportunities built into the model for substituting one factor of production for another. In simple versions of the CGE model, this means looking at the supply of and demand for capital as well as labor. It is widely recognized that labor and capital are complements as well as substitutes. Although labor and capital can, to some extent, be substituted for one another (as when a company buys a machine that reduces the number of employees needed to make a product), it is also the case that workers need machines to work with and machine owners need workers to operate the machines. In general, the more capital workers have to work with, the more productive labor will be. Conversely, the more labor there is, the more productive capital will be. Thus, regulation can reduce labor employment and wages indirectly as well as directly, by reducing the amount of capital employed.

More complicated general equilibrium models entail various additional refinements, taking into account effects relating to any or all of the following types of factors, among others:

• interconnections between different sectors of the economy (e.g., between the energy sector and all other sectors) that cause regulation of one sector to affect every other sector to one degree or another;

- ability of firms to substitute capital for labor, and of workers to substitute leisure or work in the unregulated household sector, if the regulation/tax wedge on labor increases;
- complementarity between capital and labor, such that regulation-induced reductions in the amount of capital that workers have to work with can reduce the growth of productivity, wages, and employment levels over time;
- changes in savings, investment, and capital formation over time within the domestic economy;
- international capital (and sometimes labor) flows.

For the purpose of addressing the employment effects of some regulations, such as the minimum wage, an adequate model would also have to include differentiation of employees by skill categories (low, medium, high) because, in the long run, wages and employment levels for medium- and high-skilled labor depend on how much capital and low-skilled labor are available to interact with and complement medium- and high-skilled labor.

Just as capital and labor are complements as well as substitutes, so different kinds and qualities of labor are complements as well as substitutes. The models and techniques necessary to take account of these factors need not be overly complex, but they should be dynamic and, so far as possible, should account for innovation and technological change. Only general equilibrium models are capable of dealing with interconnections among different sectors of the economy, and only general equilibrium models are capable of dealing with the kinds of interactions among different regulations.

For example, producers can adjust their production technology to become more or less labor-intensive if there is a change in the relative cost of capital as compared to labor costs. Not allowing for such substitution possibilities in assessing employment effects could substantially underestimate employment shifts and the amount of temporary unemployment that would result from changes in regulation. This substitution process will also have important impacts on wages, as the ratio of capital to labor in a given sector affects worker productivity and wage rates. The extent to which this occurs is estimated statistically by using what are called substitution elasticities. (These elasticities show the extent to which one variable changes with respect to another.)

Estimates of elasticities must be assembled for primary factor (i.e., labor and capital) substitution, import demand, import source, domestic demand, and transformation of domestic supply into domestic and exported products. Since elasticity estimates are subject to a margin of error, the remedy for this problem, which is endemic to any large-scale model of this kind, is to test how sensitive the model results are with respect to plausible bounds on these elasticities. To the extent that the major conclusions from this exercise are robust to variations within these bounds, uncertainty over some specific values of these elasticities should not be construed as a weakness of the model.

How a CGE Model is Developed

A CGE model is developed by combining multisectoral data bases of an economy with computer software that simulates the functioning and reactions of the economy. The typical data base for this purpose is a social accounting matrix (SAM), which shows the transactions that take place among all agents of an economy in some base year. It essentially provides a snapshot of the economy as of some base year. The data are then applied to the model to replicate that base year in the benchmark general equilibrium.

The computer software that simulates the economy does so by assuming that production and consumption activities follow certain mathematical forms. These are production functions showing how technology determines the way in which goods can be produced using factors such as labor and capital, and utility functions showing how different combinations of goods and services generate well-being for consumers.

The particular functions adopted at this stage can be a crucial determinant of the results of a CGE model. Therefore, it is important to undertake "systematic sensitivity analysis" with respect to these functional choices. (The results of just such an analysis are shown in the next portion of this section.) Thus, it is possible to determine that the welfare or employment effects of a certain regulatory policy are bounded within certain intervals with a 75 percent confidence level. In this way the results from the model reflect the uncertainty underlying the construction of the model, rather than conveying a false and dangerous image of certainty.

A CGE model is either developed specially for some policy application or is developed for a range of applications. The choice between these two is largely a matter of the budget that can be allocated to the modeling exercise. A cost-effective procedure is to modify an existing CGE model to reflect the concerns of policymakers in a particular setting. There are obvious limits on how completely one can modify existing CGE models in a limited time frame, but modern advances in software do make such modifications much easier than in the past.

How to Use a CGE Model

A CGE model is used in a policy setting by first deciding carefully on how the regulatory policy is to be modeled. The next step is to collect data on the changes in the affected elements of the economy from an econometric estimate or from a survey designed for the purpose. The final step is to decipher and interpret the detailed output that results. The last step should not be minimized, since in a policy framework one is often generating results to meet a deadline, leaving little time to assess all of the effects that a policy may have. In such a circumstance it is all the more important to have a model that is constructed using standard and accepted economic foundations.

MODELING REGULATORY POLICY

Analysts of regulatory policy customarily distinguish between two broad categories of regulatory activity: economic regulation and social regulation. These major types of regulation each produce different types of social and economic impacts, and the proper modeling of these effects can be crucial when evaluating them in a CGE framework.

There will always be adjustment costs in terms of labor relocations and possible unemployment from any change in regulation, whether it is the imposition of new regulations or elimination of existing regulations. Yet, regulation per se does not have to lead to permanently higher unemployment levels. In the absence of labor market rigidities and distortions that inhibit the wage level from adjusting to changing market conditions, unemployment would simply be a result of friction in the job search process. To a large extent, therefore, changes in unemployment will be caused by changing regulatory policies and not the existence of such policies. The same cannot be concluded with respect to wage rates. With fully flexible labor markets, the mere existence of regulatory policies may cause a permanent drop in real wages (discussed later).

If one were to model only the costs of regulatory policy, and not the possible benefits, then one would be setting up a disingenuous analysis of potential impacts. Thus, it is incumbent on those who study regulatory policies to try to explain clearly how the policy is supposed to affect benefits as well as how it imposes costs on the economy and society. If a model is unable to encompass behavior that leads to alleged benefits from regulation, then either the economic basis for those alleged benefits may be questioned or the model itself may be inappropriate to assess the costs.

A great deal of current regulatory activity in the United States concerns the delineation of standards for businesses and industry. These standards refer to a wide variety of activities, including production processes that have environmental effects, health and safety issues in the workplace, and consideration of civil rights in employment. To use a CGE model to assess regulatory impacts, one must first assume that data are available to show estimated expenditures in each sector to comply with a mandated regulatory standard. Admittedly, these data will be difficult to obtain.

How can these data on regulatory compliance expenditures be used in a CGE model? The approach used here is to postulate the existence of a "risk reduction" activity for each employment sector. This allows description of activities that, for example, reduce environmental risk through the employment of pollution abatement technologies, or activities that reduce health risks through the employment of safety equipment. Regulation then can be interpreted as a requirement on industry to undertake certain "risk-reducing" activities in order to produce. These activities give rise to compliance expenditures, as noted. Using this approach assumes the existence of data on expenditures incurred at the sectoral level, to comply with the regulated risk-reducing activity.

In the model, regulatory requirements are assumed to be the sole reason that industries engage in these activities. Thus, in the absence of such regulation one could expect a complete elimination of expenditures on these activities. This assumption allows modeling the employment effects of alternative levels and approaches to regulatory activities by simply relaxing the required amount of risk-reducing activities that are necessary to receive permission to produce. As the requirement is reduced, the firms in each sector can produce more cheaply by not having to incur regulatory compliance costs. Similarly, increasing the risk-reduction requirement can be interpreted as the effect of tightening regulations.

Easing the risk-reduction requirement for an industry is, therefore, more likely to increase the employment level in the industry. Simultaneously, however, there will be reductions in the employment of labor in risk-reducing activities, such as the manufacture and installation of safety and control devices. Overall, one would expect a temporary rise in unemployment after either a reduction or an increase in requirements; however, the real wage level is more likely to fall with increases rather than with reductions in regulation. The advantage of this approach to modeling employment effects of regulation is that one can evaluate the effects of across-the-board changes in regulation in the same framework as one evaluates any sectoral changes.

HOW TO MODEL LABOR MARKETS

A number of employment issues can be analyzed as they relate to changes in regulatory policies in the simple model employed here. One major concern is, of course, effects on the aggregate rate of unemployment. Other concerns relate to sectoral employment impacts and changes in the wage rate.

Unemployment

Changing sectoral employment patterns that emerge as a result of regulatory actions are a major cause of changes in the frictional unemployment rate. Unemployment is a feature of competitive labor markets because such markets are inherently dynamic and because the characteristics of those looking for work and the nature of the jobs offered are not necessarily equivalent. This causes frictional unemployment due to the search activities that have to be performed by both employers and workers.

Frictional unemployment is bound to be temporary in the absence of labor market rigidities and distortions, as eventually the wage rate will adjust and both employers and workers will find a matching partner. A decrease in employment in any one sector must, through the changing wage rate, eventually be absorbed by expanding employment somewhere else in the economy.

If, for example, a change in regulatory requirements for pollution abatement causes 3 percent of the labor force to have to relocate across sectors, a large part of this labor force will, at least temporarily, be classified as unemployed as it searches for employment in expanding sectors. This allows an interpretation of sectoral employment impacts after a change in regulation.

It would be quite easy to extend a model in order to evaluate the employment impact on different types of labor separately. Occupational categories, such as management and professional, technical, sales and administrative support, service occupations, precision production, craft and repair, farming, forestry and fishing, and operators, fabricators and laborers could easily be identified.

Permanent or structural changes in the aggregate employment level would only arise if there are inherent rigidities and distortions in the labor market that prohibit wages from adjusting fully and allowing the economy to return to full employment. Evaluating employment effects in a more precise and sophisticated manner in order to capture structural unemployment effects will require careful consideration of the exact mechanisms by which employment and wages adjust.

Consider, for example, the fact that union wages, which are usually higher than nonunion wages, introduce distortions that could cause structural unemployment. If wages are not allowed to fall after a large increase in unemployment, the demand for labor will not increase and extended periods of unemployment will result. Other rigidities elsewhere in the system, stemming from factors such as unemployment insurance benefits, have the effect of lowering the cost to workers of remaining unemployed and, therefore, allowing extended job search time and prolonged unemployment periods.

Unemployment could also be due to wage differentials across employment sectors, even in the absence of explicit and implicit wage floors and unionism. The existence of a wage premium in some employment sectors gives individuals an incentive to remain unemployed and queue for high-wage jobs in those sectors. As long as the expected wage from choosing to wait for a job in the high-wage sectors exceeds the expected wage from searching for work while unemployed, workers will choose to opt for unemployment.

Similarly, unemployment among low-skilled workers is likely to be prevalent if employers pay above market-clearing wages to cut down on worker shirking and to increase productivity. This latter type of unemployment could also occur as a result of minimum wage legislation.

It is clear that there are a number of reasons why the permanent unemployment rate might be positive. The important thing to recognize in terms of modeling this type of unemployment is that both its magnitude and the direction of change as a result of changing regulatory policies depend crucially on the particular assumptions employed in the model.

Wages

In addition to analyzing employment shifts, the CGE model can also estimate the expected impact on wages from proposed regulatory actions. As was the case for structural unemployment, the exact modeling of labor markets will determine what results can be expected in terms of changes in wages.

For example, the modelling of wage differentials across industries can take several forms and result in quite different effects on wages, in terms of both magnitudes and directions of change. Some wage differentials are due to observable differences in worker characteristics, such as education and work experience. Those differentials are easily captured in most modeling exercises, at least if they are treated as fixed and independent of the regulatory process.

More difficulties arise if wage differentials are due to statistically unobserved differences such as differences in work ethics among workers, or if they are not fixed and independent of the regulatory process. It is important in any modeling exercise, not just in CGE models, to recognize the potential impact of different labor market assumptions. The CGE method can, in general, investigate wage and employment effects on the basis of any of these labor market assumptions. It is also possible to compute a range of results in order to evaluate the confidence one might have in terms of particular results.

The advantage of CGE modeling over other analytical tools for assessing regulatory impacts lies in its flexibility for adapting to a variety of assumptions, capacity for incorporating linkages across contracting and expanding employment sectors, and completeness in terms of including all the links that exist across households and employment sectors.

Executive Order 12866 of September 30, 1993—Regulatory Planning and Review

The American people deserve a regulatory system that works for them, not against them: a regulatory system that protects and improves their health, safety, environment, and well-being and improves the performance of the economy without imposing unacceptable or unreasonable costs on society; regulatory policies that recognize that the private sector and private markets are the best engine for economic growth; regulatory approaches that respect the role of State, local, and tribal governments; and regulations that are effective, consistent, sensible, and understandable. We do not have such a regulatory system today.

With this Executive order, the Federal Government begins a program to reform and make more efficient the regulatory process. The objectives of this Executive order are to enhance planning and coordination with respect to both new and existing regulations; to reaffirm the primacy of Federal agencies in the regulatory decision-making process; to restore the integrity and legitimacy of regulatory review and oversight; and to make the process more accessible and open to the public. In pursuing these objectives, the regulatory process shall be conducted so as to meet applicable statutory requirements and with due regard to the discretion that has been entrusted to the Federal agencies.

Accordingly, by the authority vested in me as President by the Constitution and the laws of the United States of America, it is hereby ordered as follows:

Section 1. *Statement of Regulatory Philosophy and Principles.* (a) *The Regulatory Philosophy.* Federal agencies should promulgate only such regulations as are required by law, are necessary to interpret the law, or are made necessary by compelling public need, such as material failures of private markets to protect or improve the health and safety of the public, the environment, or the well-being of the American people. In deciding whether and how to regulate, agencies should assess all costs and benefits of available regulatory alternatives, including the alternative of not regulating. Costs and benefits shall be understood to include both quantifiable measures (to the fullest extent that these can be usefully estimated) and qualitative measures of costs and benefits that are difficult to quantify, but nevertheless essential to consider. Further, in choosing among alternative regulatory approaches, agencies should select those approaches that maximize net benefits (including potential economic, environmental, public health and safety, and other advantages; distributive impacts; and equity), unless a statute requires another regulatory approach.

(b) *The Principles of Regulation.* To ensure that the agencies' regulatory programs are consistent with the philosophy set forth above, agencies should adhere to the following principles, to the extent permitted by law and where applicable:

(1) Each agency shall identify the problem that it intends to address (including, where applicable, the failures of private markets or public institutions that warrant new agency action) as well as assess the significance of that problem.

(2) Each agency shall examine whether existing regulations (or other law) have created, or contributed to, the problem that a new regulation is intended to correct and whether those regulations (or other law) should be modified to achieve the intended goal of regulation more effectively.

(3) Each agency shall identify and assess available alternatives to direct regulation, including providing economic incentives to encourage the desired behavior, such as user fees or marketable permits, or providing information upon which choices can be made by the public.

(4) In setting regulatory priorities, each agency shall consider, to the extent reasonable, the degree and nature of the risks posed by various substances or activities within its jurisdiction.

(5) When an agency determines that a regulation is the best available method of achieving the regulatory objective, it shall design its regulations in the most cost-effective manner to achieve the regulatory objective. In doing so, each agency shall consider incentives for innovation, consistency, predictability, the costs of enforcement and compliance (to the government, regulated entities, and the public), flexibility, distributive impacts, and equity.

(6) Each agency shall assess both the costs and the benefits of the intended regulation and, recognizing that some costs and benefits are difficult to quantify, propose or adopt a regulation only upon a reasoned determination that the benefits of the intended regulation justify its costs.

(7) Each agency shall base its decisions on the best reasonably obtainable scientific, technical, economic, and other information concerning the need for, and consequences of, the intended regulation.

(8) Each agency shall identify and assess alternative forms of regulation and shall, to the extent feasible, specify performance objectives, rather than specifying the behavior or manner of compliance that regulated entities must adopt.

(9) Wherever feasible, agencies shall seek views of appropriate State, local, and tribal officials before imposing regulatory requirements that might significantly or uniquely affect those governmental entities. Each agency shall assess the effects of Federal regulations on State, local, and tribal governments, including specifically the availability of resources to carry out those mandates, and seek to minimize those burdens that uniquely or significantly affect such governmental entities, consistent with achieving regulatory objectives. In addition, as appropriate, agencies shall seek to harmonize Federal regulatory actions with related State, local, and tribal regulatory and other governmental functions.

(10) Each agency shall avoid regulations that are inconsistent, incompatible, or duplicative with its other regulations or those of other Federal agencies.

(11) Each agency shall tailor its regulations to impose the least burden on society, including individuals, businesses of differing sizes, and other entities (including small communities and governmental entities), consistent with obtaining the regulatory objectives, taking into account, among other things, and to the extent practicable, the costs of cumulative regulations.

(12) Each agency shall draft its regulations to be simple and easy to understand, with the goal of minimizing the potential for uncertainty and litigation arising from such uncertainty.

Sec. 2. *Organization.* An efficient regulatory planning and review process is vital to ensure that the Federal Government's regulatory system best serves the American people.

(a) *The Agencies.* Because Federal agencies are the repositories of significant substantive expertise and experience, they are responsible for developing regulations and assuring that the regulations are consistent with applicable law, the President's priorities, and the principles set forth in this Executive order.

(b) *The Office of Management and Budget.* Coordinated review of agency rulemaking is necessary to ensure that regulations are consistent with applicable law, the President's priorities, and the principles set forth in this Executive order, and that decisions made by one agency do not conflict with the policies or actions taken or planned by another agency. The Office of Management and Budget (OMB) shall carry out that review function. Within OMB, the Office of Information and Regulatory Affairs (OIRA) is the repository of expertise concerning regulatory issues, including methodologies and procedures that affect more than one agency, this Executive order, and the President's regulatory policies. To the extent permitted by law, OMB shall provide guidance to agencies and assist the President, the Vice President, and other regulatory policy advisors to the President in regulatory planning and shall be the entity that reviews individual regulations, as provided by this Executive order.

(c) *The Vice President.* The Vice President is the principal advisor to the President on, and shall coordinate the development and presentation of recommendations concerning, regulatory policy, planning, and review, as set forth in this Executive order. In fulfilling their responsibilities under this Executive order, the President and the Vice President shall be assisted by the regulatory policy advisors within the Executive Office of the President and by such agency officials and personnel as the President and the Vice President may, from time to time, consult.

Sec. 3. *Definitions.* For purposes of this Executive order: (a) "Advisors" refers to such regulatory policy advisors to the President as the President and Vice President may from time to time consult, including, among others: (1) the Director of OMB; (2) the Chair (or another member) of the Council of Economic Advisers; (3) the Assistant to the President for Economic Policy; (4) the Assistant to the President for Domestic Policy; (5) the Assistant to the President for National Security Affairs; (6) the Assistant to the President for Science and Technology; (7) the Assistant to the President for Intergovernmental Affairs; (8) the Assistant to the President and Staff Secretary; (9) the Assistant to the President and Chief of Staff to the Vice President; (10) the Assistant to the President and Counsel to the President; (11) the Deputy Assistant to the President and Director of the White House Office on Environmental Policy; and (12) the Administrator of OIRA, who also shall coordinate communications relating to this Executive order among the agencies, OMB, the other Advisors, and the Office of the Vice President.

(b) "Agency," unless otherwise indicated, means any authority of the United States that is an "agency" under 44 U.S.C. 3502(1), other than those considered to be independent regulatory agencies, as defined in 44 U.S.C. 3502(10).

(c) "Director" means the Director of OMB.

(d) "Regulation" or "rule" means an agency statement of general applicability and future effect, which the agency intends to have the force and effect of law, that is designed to implement, interpret, or prescribe law or policy or to describe the procedure or practice requirements of an agency. It does not, however, include:

(1) Regulations or rules issued in accordance with the formal rulemaking provisions of 5 U.S.C. 556, 557;

(2) Regulations or rules that pertain to a military or foreign affairs function of the United States, other than procurement regulations and regulations involving the import or export of non-defense articles and services;

(3) Regulations or rules that are limited to agency organization, management, or personnel matters; or

(4) Any other category of regulations exempted by the Administrator of OIRA.

(e) "Regulatory action" means any substantive action by an agency (normally published in the **Federal Register**) that promulgates or is expected to lead to the promulgation of a final rule or regulation, including notices of inquiry, advance notices of proposed rulemaking, and notices of proposed rulemaking.

(f) "Significant regulatory action" means any regulatory action that is likely to result in a rule that may:

(1) Have an annual effect on the economy of $100 million or more or adversely affect in a material way the economy, a sector of the economy, productivity, competition, jobs, the environment, public health or safety, or State, local, or tribal governments or communities;

(2) Create a serious inconsistency or otherwise interfere with an action taken or planned by another agency;

(3) Materially alter the budgetary impact of entitlements, grants, user fees, or loan programs or the rights and obligations of recipients thereof; or

(4) Raise novel legal or policy issues arising out of legal mandates, the President's priorities, or the principles set forth in this Executive order.

Sec. 4. *Planning Mechanism.* In order to have an effective regulatory program, to provide for coordination of regulations, to maximize consultation and the resolution of potential conflicts at an early stage, to involve the public and its State, local, and tribal officials in regulatory planning, and to ensure that new or revised regulations promote the President's priorities and the principles set forth in this Executive order, these procedures shall be followed, to the extent permitted by law: (a) *Agencies' Policy Meeting.* Early in each year's planning cycle, the Vice President shall convene a meeting of the Advisors and the heads of agencies to seek a common understanding of priorities and to coordinate regulatory efforts to be accomplished in the upcoming year.

(b) *Unified Regulatory Agenda.* For purposes of this subsection, the term "agency" or "agencies" shall also include those considered to be independent regulatory agencies, as defined in 44 U.S.C. 3502(10). Each agency shall prepare an agenda of all regulations under development or review, at a time and in a manner specified by the Administrator of OIRA. The description of each regulatory action shall contain, at a minimum, a regulation identifier number, a brief summary of the action, the legal authority for the action, any legal deadline for the action, and the name and telephone number of a knowledgeable agency official. Agencies may incorporate the information required under 5 U.S.C. 602 and 41 U.S.C. 402 into these agendas.

(c) *The Regulatory Plan.* For purposes of this subsection, the term "agency" or "agencies" shall also include those considered to be independent regulatory agencies, as defined in 44 U.S.C. 3502(10). (1) As part of the Unified Regulatory Agenda, beginning in 1994, each agency shall prepare a Regulatory

Plan (Plan) of the most important significant regulatory actions that the agency reasonably expects to issue in proposed or final form in that fiscal year or thereafter. The Plan shall be approved personally by the agency head and shall contain at a minimum:

(A) A statement of the agency's regulatory objectives and priorities and how they relate to the President's priorities;

(B) A summary of each planned significant regulatory action including, to the extent possible, alternatives to be considered and preliminary estimates of the anticipated costs and benefits;

(C) A summary of the legal basis for each such action, including whether any aspect of the action is required by statute or court order;

(D) A statement of the need for each such action and, if applicable, how the action will reduce risks to public health, safety, or the environment, as well as how the magnitude of the risk addressed by the action relates to other risks within the jurisdiction of the agency;

(E) The agency's schedule for action, including a statement of any applicable statutory or judicial deadlines; and

(F) The name, address, and telephone number of a person the public may contact for additional information about the planned regulatory action.

(2) Each agency shall forward its Plan to OIRA by June 1st of each year.

(3) Within 10 calendar days after OIRA has received an agency's Plan, OIRA shall circulate it to other affected agencies, the Advisors, and the Vice President.

(4) An agency head who believes that a planned regulatory action of another agency may conflict with its own policy or action taken or planned shall promptly notify, in writing, the Administrator of OIRA, who shall forward that communication to the issuing agency, the Advisors, and the Vice President.

(5) If the Administrator of OIRA believes that a planned regulatory action of an agency may be inconsistent with the President's priorities or the principles set forth in this Executive order or may be in conflict with any policy or action taken or planned by another agency, the Administrator of OIRA shall promptly notify, in writing, the affected agencies, the Advisors, and the Vice President.

(6) The Vice President, with the Advisors' assistance, may consult with the heads of agencies with respect to their Plans and, in appropriate instances, request further consideration or inter-agency coordination.

(7) The Plans developed by the issuing agency shall be published annually in the October publication of the Unified Regulatory Agenda. This publication shall be made available to the Congress; State, local, and tribal governments; and the public. Any views on any aspect of any agency Plan, including whether any planned regulatory action might conflict with any other planned or existing regulation, impose any unintended consequences

on the public, or confer any unclaimed benefits on the public, should be directed to the issuing agency, with a copy to OIRA.

(d) *Regulatory Working Group.* Within 30 days of the date of this Executive order, the Administrator of OIRA shall convene a Regulatory Working Group ("Working Group"), which shall consist of representatives of the heads of each agency that the Administrator determines to have significant domestic regulatory responsibility, the Advisors, and the Vice President. The Administrator of OIRA shall chair the Working Group and shall periodically advise the Vice President on the activities of the Working Group. The Working Group shall serve as a forum to assist agencies in identifying and analyzing important regulatory issues (including, among others (1) the development of innovative regulatory techniques, (2) the methods, efficacy, and utility of comparative risk assessment in regulatory decision-making, and (3) the development of short forms and other streamlined regulatory approaches for small businesses and other entities). The Working Group shall meet at least quarterly and may meet as a whole or in subgroups of agencies with an interest in particular issues or subject areas. To inform its discussions, the Working Group may commission analytical studies and reports by OIRA, the Administrative Conference of the United States, or any other agency.

(e) *Conferences.* The Administrator of OIRA shall meet quarterly with representatives of State, local, and tribal governments to identify both existing and proposed regulations that may uniquely or significantly affect those governmental entities. The Administrator of OIRA shall also convene, from time to time, conferences with representatives of businesses, nongovernmental organizations, and the public to discuss regulatory issues of common concern.

Sec. 5. *Existing Regulations.* In order to reduce the regulatory burden on the American people, their families, their communities, their State, local, and tribal governments, and their industries; to determine whether regulations promulgated by the executive branch of the Federal Government have become unjustified or unnecessary as a result of changed circumstances; to confirm that regulations are both compatible with each other and not duplicative or inappropriately burdensome in the aggregate; to ensure that all regulations are consistent with the President's priorities and the principles set forth in this Executive order, within applicable law; and to otherwise improve the effectiveness of existing regulations: (a) Within 90 days of the date of this Executive order, each agency shall submit to OIRA a program, consistent with its resources and regulatory priorities, under which the agency will periodically review its existing significant regulations to determine whether any such regulations should be modified or eliminated so as to make the agency's regulatory program more effective in achieving the regulatory objectives, less burdensome, or in greater alignment with the President's priorities and the principles set forth in this Executive order. Any significant regulations selected for review shall be included in the agency's annual Plan. The agency shall also identify any legislative mandates that require the agency to promulgate or continue to impose regulations that the agency believes are unnecessary or outdated by reason of changed circumstances.

(b) The Administrator of OIRA shall work with the Regulatory Working Group and other interested entities to pursue the objectives of this section. State, local, and tribal governments are specifically encouraged to assist in the identification of regulations that impose significant or unique burdens on those governmental entities and that appear to have outlived their justification or be otherwise inconsistent with the public interest.

(c) The Vice President, in consultation with the Advisors, may identify for review by the appropriate agency or agencies other existing regulations of an agency or groups of regulations of more than one agency that affect a particular group, industry, or sector of the economy, or may identify legislative mandates that may be appropriate for reconsideration by the Congress.

Sec. 6. *Centralized Review of Regulations.* The guidelines set forth below shall apply to all regulatory actions, for both new and existing regulations, by agencies other than those agencies specifically exempted by the Administrator of OIRA:

(a) *Agency Responsibilities.* (1) Each agency shall (consistent with its own rules, regulations, or procedures) provide the public with meaningful participation in the regulatory process. In particular, before issuing a notice of proposed rulemaking, each agency should, where appropriate, seek the involvement of those who are intended to benefit from and those expected to be burdened by any regulation (including, specifically, State, local, and tribal officials). In addition, each agency should afford the public a meaningful opportunity to comment on any proposed regulation, which in most cases should include a comment period of not less than 60 days. Each agency also is directed to explore and, where appropriate, use consensual mechanisms for developing regulations, including negotiated rulemaking.

(2) Within 60 days of the date of this Executive order, each agency head shall designate a Regulatory Policy Officer who shall report to the agency head. The Regulatory Policy Officer shall be involved at each stage of the regulatory process to foster the development of effective, innovative, and least burdensome regulations and to further the principles set forth in this Executive order.

(3) In addition to adhering to its own rules and procedures and to the requirements of the Administrative Procedure Act, the Regulatory Flexibility Act, the Paperwork Reduction Act, and other applicable law, each agency shall develop its regulatory actions in a timely fashion and adhere to the following procedures with respect to a regulatory action:

(A) Each agency shall provide OIRA, at such times and in the manner specified by the Administrator of OIRA, with a list of its planned regulatory actions, indicating those which the agency believes are significant regulatory actions within the meaning of this Executive order. Absent a material change in the development of the planned regulatory action, those not designated as significant will not be subject to review under this section unless, within 10 working days of receipt of the list, the Administrator of OIRA notifies the agency that OIRA has determined that a planned regulation is a significant regulatory action within the meaning of this Executive order. The Administrator of OIRA may waive review of any planned regulatory action designated by the agency as significant, in which case the agency need not further comply with subsection (a)(3)(B) or subsection (a)(3)(C) of this section.

(B) For each matter identified as, or determined by the Administrator of OIRA to be, a significant regulatory action, the issuing agency shall provide to OIRA:

(i) The text of the draft regulatory action, together with a reasonably detailed description of the need for the regulatory action and an explanation of how the regulatory action will meet that need; and

(ii) An assessment of the potential costs and benefits of the regulatory action, including an explanation of the manner in which the regulatory action is consistent with a statutory mandate and, to the extent permitted by law, promotes the President's priorities and avoids undue interference with State, local, and tribal governments in the exercise of their governmental functions.

(C) For those matters identified as, or determined by the Administrator of OIRA to be, a significant regulatory action within the scope of section 3(f)(1), the agency shall also provide to OIRA the following additional information developed as part of the agency's decision-making process (unless prohibited by law):

(i) An assessment, including the underlying analysis, of benefits anticipated from the regulatory action (such as, but not limited to, the promotion of the efficient functioning of the economy and private markets, the enhancement of health and safety, the protection of the natural environment, and the elimination or reduction of discrimination or bias) together with, to the extent feasible, a quantification of those benefits;

(ii) An assessment, including the underlying analysis, of costs anticipated from the regulatory action (such as, but not limited to, the direct cost both to the government in administering the regulation and to businesses and others in complying with the regulation, and any adverse effects on the efficient functioning of the economy, private markets (including productivity, employment, and competitiveness), health, safety, and the natural environment), together with, to the extent feasible, a quantification of those costs; and

(iii) An assessment, including the underlying analysis, of costs and benefits of potentially effective and reasonably feasible alternatives to the planned regulation, identified by the agencies or the public (including improving the current regulation and reasonably viable nonregulatory actions), and an explanation why the planned regulatory action is preferable to the identified potential alternatives.

(D) In emergency situations or when an agency is obligated by law to act more quickly than normal review procedures allow, the agency shall notify OIRA as soon as possible and, to the extent practicable, comply with subsections (a)(3)(B) and (C) of this section. For those regulatory actions that are governed by a statutory or court-imposed deadline, the agency shall, to the extent practicable, schedule rulemaking proceedings so as to permit sufficient time for OIRA to conduct its review, as set forth below in subsection (b)(2) through (4) of this section.

(E) After the regulatory action has been published in the **Federal Register** or otherwise issued to the public, the agency shall:

(i) Make available to the public the information set forth in subsections (a)(3)(B) and (C);

(ii) Identify for the public, in a complete, clear, and simple manner, the substantive changes between the draft submitted to OIRA for review and the action subsequently announced; and

(iii) Identify for the public those changes in the regulatory action that were made at the suggestion or recommendation of OIRA.

(F) All information provided to the public by the agency shall be in plain, understandable language.

(b) *OIRA Responsibilities.* The Administrator of OIRA shall provide meaningful guidance and oversight so that each agency's regulatory actions are consistent with applicable law, the President's priorities, and the principles set forth in this Executive order and do not conflict with the policies or actions of another agency. OIRA shall, to the extent permitted by law, adhere to the following guidelines:

(1) OIRA may review only actions identified by the agency or by OIRA as significant regulatory actions under subsection (a)(3)(A) of this section.

(2) OIRA shall waive review or notify the agency in writing of the results of its review within the following time periods:

(A) For any notices of inquiry, advance notices of proposed rulemaking, or other preliminary regulatory actions prior to a Notice of Proposed Rulemaking, within 10 working days after the date of submission of the draft action to OIRA;

(B) For all other regulatory actions, within 90 calendar days after the date of submission of the information set forth in subsections (a)(3)(B) and (C) of this section, unless OIRA has previously reviewed this information and, since that review, there has been no material change in the facts and circumstances upon which the regulatory action is based, in which case, OIRA shall complete its review within 45 days; and

(C) The review process may be extended (1) once by no more than 30 calendar days upon the written approval of the Director and (2) at the request of the agency head.

(3) For each regulatory action that the Administrator of OIRA returns to an agency for further consideration of some or all of its provisions, the Administrator of OIRA shall provide the issuing agency a written explanation for such return, setting forth the pertinent provision of this Executive order on which OIRA is relying. If the agency head disagrees with some or all of the bases for the return, the agency head shall so inform the Administrator of OIRA in writing.

(4) Except as otherwise provided by law or required by a Court, in order to ensure greater openness, accessibility, and accountability in the regulatory review process, OIRA shall be governed by the following disclosure requirements:

(A) Only the Administrator of OIRA (or a particular designee) shall receive oral communications initiated by persons not employed by the executive branch of the Federal Government regarding the substance of a regulatory action under OIRA review;

(B) All substantive communications between OIRA personnel and persons not employed by the executive branch of the Federal Government regarding a regulatory action under review shall be governed by the following guidelines: (i) A representative from the issuing agency shall be invited to any meeting between OIRA personnel and such person(s):

(ii) OIRA shall forward to the issuing agency within 10 working days of receipt of the communication(s), all written communications, regardless of format, between OIRA personnel and any person who is not employed by the executive branch of the Federal Government, and the dates and names of individuals involved in all substantive oral communications (including meetings to which an agency representative was invited, but did not attend, and telephone conversations between OIRA personnel and any such persons); and

(iii) OIRA shall publicly disclose relevant information about such communication(s), as set forth below in subsection (b)(4)(C) of this section.

(C) OIRA shall maintain a publicly available log that shall contain, at a minimum, the following information pertinent to regulatory actions under review:

(i) The status of all regulatory actions, including if (and if so, when and by whom) Vice Presidential and Presidential consideration was requested;

(ii) A notation of all written communications forwarded to an issuing agency under subsection (b)(4)(B)(ii) of this section; and

(iii) The dates and names of individuals involved in all substantive oral communications, including meetings and telephone conversations, between OIRA personnel and any person not employed by the executive branch of the Federal Government, and the subject matter discussed during such communications.

(D) After the regulatory action has been published in the **Federal Register** or otherwise issued to the public, or after the agency has announced its decision not to publish or issue the regulatory action, OIRA shall make available to the public all documents exchanged between OIRA and the agency during the review by OIRA under this section.

(5) All information provided to the public by OIRA shall be in plain, understandable language.

Sec. 7. *Resolution of Conflicts.* To the extent permitted by law, disagreements or conflicts between or among agency heads or between OMB and any agency that cannot be resolved by the Administrator of OIRA shall be resolved by the President, or by the Vice President acting at the request of the President, with the relevant agency head (and, as appropriate, other interested government officials). Vice Presidential and Presidential consideration of such disagreements may be initiated only by the Director, by the head of the issuing agency, or by the head of an agency that has a significant interest in the regulatory action at issue. Such review will not be undertaken at the request of other persons, entities, or their agents.

Resolution of such conflicts shall be informed by recommendations developed by the Vice President, after consultation with the Advisors (and other executive branch officials or personnel whose responsibilities to the President include the subject matter at issue). The development of these recommendations shall be concluded within 60 days after review has been requested.

During the Vice Presidential and Presidential review period, communications with any person not employed by the Federal Government relating to the substance of the regulatory action under review and directed to the Advisors or their staffs or to the staff of the Vice President shall be in writing and shall be forwarded by the recipient to the affected agency(ies) for inclusion in the public docket(s). When the communication is not in writing, such Advisors or staff members shall inform the outside party that the matter is under review and that any comments should be submitted in writing.

At the end of this review process, the President, or the Vice President acting at the request of the President, shall notify the affected agency and the Administrator of OIRA of the President's decision with respect to the matter.

Sec. 8. *Publication.* Except to the extent required by law, an agency shall not publish in the **Federal Register** or otherwise issue to the public any regulatory action that is subject to review under section 6 of this Executive order until (1) the Administrator of OIRA notifies the agency that OIRA has waived its review of the action or has completed its review without any requests for further consideration, or (2) the applicable time period in section 6(b)(2) expires without OIRA having notified the agency that it is returning the regulatory action for further consideration under section 6(b)(3), whichever occurs first. If the terms of the preceding sentence have not been satisfied and an agency wants to publish or otherwise issue a regulatory action, the head of that agency may request Presidential consideration through the Vice President, as provided under section 7 of this order. Upon receipt of this request, the Vice President shall notify OIRA and the Advisors. The guidelines and time period set forth in section 7 shall apply to the publication of regulatory actions for which Presidential consideration has been sought.

Sec. 9. *Agency Authority.* Nothing in this order shall be construed as displacing the agencies' authority or responsibilities, as authorized by law.

Sec. 10. *Judicial Review.* Nothing in this Executive order shall affect any otherwise available judicial review of agency action. This Executive order is intended only to improve the internal management of the Federal Government and does not create any right or benefit, substantive or procedural, enforceable at law or equity by a party against the United States, its agencies or instrumentalities, its officers or employees, or any other person.

Sec. 11. *Revocations.* Executive Orders Nos. 12291 and 12498; all amendments to those Executive orders; all guidelines issued under those orders; and any exemptions from those orders heretofore granted for any category of rule are revoked.

William J Clinton

THE WHITE HOUSE,
September 30, 1993.

Editorial note: For the President's remarks on signing this Executive order, see issue 39 of the *Weekly Compilation of Presidential Documents.*

Appendix C
Excerpts from "Economic Analysis of Federal Regulations Under Executive Order 12866"— January 11, 1996

INTRODUCTION

In accordance with the regulatory philosophy and principles provided in Sections 1(a) and (b) and Section 6(a)(3)(C) of Executive Order 12866, an Economic Analysis (EA) of proposed or existing regulations should inform decisionmakers of the consequences of alternative actions. In particular, the EA should provide information allowing decisionmakers to determine that:

- There is adequate information indicating the need for and consequences of the proposed action;
- The potential benefits to society justify the potential costs, recognizing that not all benefits and costs can be described in monetary or even in quantitative terms, unless a statute requires another regulatory approach;
- The proposed action will maximize net benefits to society (including potential economic, environmental, public health and safety, and other advantages; distributional impacts; and equity), unless a statute requires another regulatory approach;
- Where a statute requires a specific regulatory approach, the proposed action will be the most cost-effective, including reliance on performance objectives to the extent feasible;
- Agency decisions are based on the best reasonably obtainable scientific, technical, economic, and other information.

While most EAs should include these elements, variations consistent with the spirit and intent of the Executive Order may be warranted for some regulatory actions. In particular, regulations establishing terms or conditions of Federal grants, contracts, or financial assistance may call for a different form of regulatory analysis, although a full-blown benefit-cost analysis of the entire program may be appropriate to inform Congress and the President more fully about its desirability.

The EA that the agency prepares should also satisfy the requirements of the "Unfunded Mandates Reform Act of 1995" (P.L. 104–4). Title II of this statute (Section 201) directs agencies "unless otherwise prohibited by law [to] assess the effects of Federal regulatory actions on State, local, and tribal governments, and the private sector." Section 202(a) directs agencies to provide a qualitative and quantitative assessment of the anticipated costs and benefits of a Federal mandate resulting in annual expenditures of $100 million or more, including the costs and benefits to State, local, and tribal governments or the private sector. Section 205(a) requires that for those regulations for which an agency prepares a statement under Section 202, "the agency shall [1] identify and consider a reasonable number of regulatory alternatives and [2] from those alternatives select the least costly, most cost-effective or least burdensome alternative that achieves the objectives of the proposed rule." If the agency does not select "the least costly, most cost-effective, or least burdensome option, and if the requirements of Section 205(a) are not "inconsistent with law," Section 205(b) requires that the agency head publish "with the final rule an explanation of why the least costly, most cost-effective, or least burdensome method was not adopted."

The "Regulatory Flexibility Act" (P.L. 96–354) requires Federal agencies to give special consideration to the impact of regulation on small businesses. The Act specifies that a regulatory flexibility analysis must be prepared if a screening analysis indicates that a regulation will have a significant impact on a substantial number of small entities. The EA that the agency prepares should incorporate the regulatory flexibility analysis, as appropriate.

This document is not in the form of a mechanistic blueprint, for a good EA cannot be written according to a formula. Competent professional judgment is indispensable for the preparation of a high-quality analysis. Different regulations may call for very different emphases in analysis. For one proposed regulation, the crucial issue may be the question of whether a market failure exists, and much of the analysis may need to be devoted to that key question. In another case, the existence of a market failure may be obvious from the outset, but extensive analysis might be necessary to estimate the magnitude of benefits to be expected from proposed regulatory alternatives.

Analysis of the risks, benefits, and costs associated with regulation must be guided by the principles of full disclosure and transparency. Data, models, inferences, and assumptions should be identified and evaluated explicitly, together with adequate justifications of choices made, and assessments of the effects of these choices on the analysis. The existence of plausible alternative models or assumptions, and their implications, should be identified. In the absence of adequate valid data, properly identified assumptions are necessary for conducting an assessment.

Preliminary and final Economic Analyses of economically "significant" rules (as defined in Section 3(f)(1) of the Executive Order) should contain three elements: (1) a statement of the need for the proposed action, (2) an examination of alternative approaches, and (3) an analysis of benefits and costs. These elements are described in Sections I–III below. The same basic analytical principles apply to the review of existing regulations, as called for under Section 5 of the Executive Order. In this case, the regulation under review should be compared to a baseline case of not taking the regulatory action and to reasonable alternatives.

I. STATEMENT OF NEED FOR THE PROPOSED ACTION

In order to establish the need for the proposed action, the analysis should discuss whether the problem constitutes a significant market failure. If the problem does not constitute a market failure, the analysis should provide an alternative demonstration of compelling public need, such as improving governmental processes or addressing distributional concerns. If the proposed action is a result of a statutory or judicial directive, that should be so stated.

A. Market Failure

The analysis should determine whether there exists a market failure that is likely to be significant. In particular, the analysis should distinguish actual market failures from potential market failures that can be resolved at relatively low cost by market participants. The major types of market failure include: externality, natural monopoly, market power, and inadequate or asymmetric information.

Government action may have unintentional harmful effects on the efficiency of market outcomes. For this reason there should be a presumption against the need for regulatory actions that, on conceptual grounds, are not expected to generate net benefits, except in special circumstances. In light of actual experience, a particularly demanding burden of proof is required to demonstrate the need for any of the following types of regulations:

- price controls in competitive markets;
- production or sales quotas in competitive markets;
- mandatory uniform quality standards for goods or services, unless they have hidden safety hazards or other defects or involve externalities and the problem cannot be adequately dealt with by voluntary standards or information disclosing the hazard to potential buyers or users; or
- controls on entry into employment or production, except (a) where indispensable to protect health and safety (e.g., FAA tests for commercial pilots) or (b) to manage the use of common property resources (e.g., fisheries, airwaves, Federal lands, and offshore areas).

B. Appropriateness of Alternatives to Federal Regulation

Even where a market failure exists, there may be no need for Federal regulatory intervention if other means of dealing with the market failure would resolve the problem adequately or better than the proposed Federal regulation would. These alternatives may include the judicial system, antitrust enforcement, and workers' compensation systems. Other nonregulatory alternatives could include, for example, subsidizing actions to achieve a desired outcome; such subsidies may be more efficient than rigid mandates. Modifications to existing regulations should be considered if those regulations have created or contributed to a problem that the new regulation is intended to correct, and if such changes can achieve the goal more efficiently or effectively. Another important factor to consider in assessing the appropriateness of a Federal regulation is regulation at the State or local level, if such an option is available.

II. AN EXAMINATION OF ALTERNATIVE APPROACHES

The EA should show that the agency has considered the most important alternative approaches to the problem and provide the agency's reasoning for selecting the proposed regulatory action over such alternatives. Ordinarily, it will be possible to eliminate some alternatives by a preliminary analysis, leaving a manageable number of alternatives to be evaluated according to the principles of the Executive Order. The number and choice of alternatives to be selected for detailed benefit-cost analysis is a matter of judgment. There must be some balance between thoroughness of analysis and practical limits to the agency's capacity to carry out analysis. With this qualifier in mind, the agency should nevertheless explore modifications of some or all of a regulation's attributes or provisions to identify appropriate alternatives.

Alternative regulatory actions that should be explored include the following:

1. More Performance-Oriented Standards for Health, Safety, and Environmental Regulations
2. Different Requirements for Different Segments of the Regulated Population
3. Alternative Levels of Stringency
4. Alternative Effective Dates of Compliance
5. Alternative Methods of Ensuring Compliance
6. Informational Measures
7. More Market-Oriented Approaches
8. Considering Specific Statutory Requirements

III. ANALYSIS OF BENEFITS AND COSTS

A. General Principles

The preliminary analysis described in Sections I and II will lead to the identification of a workable number of alternatives for consideration.

1. Baseline. The benefits and costs of each alternative must be measured against a baseline. The baseline should be the best assessment of the way the world would look absent the proposed regulation. That assessment may consider a wide range of factors, including the likely evolution of the market, likely changes in exogenous factors affecting benefits and costs, likely changes in regulations promulgated by the agency or other government entities, and the likely degree of compliance by regulated entities with other regulations. Often it may be reasonable for the agency to forecast that the world absent the regulation will resemble the present. For the review of an existing regulation, the baseline should be no change in existing regulation; this baseline can then be compared against reasonable alternatives.

When more than one baseline appears reasonable or the baseline is very uncertain, and when the estimated benefits and costs of proposed rules are likely to vary significantly with the baseline selected, the agency may choose to measure benefits and costs against multiple alternative baselines as a form of sensitivity analysis. For example, the agency may choose to conduct a sensitivity analysis involving the consequences for benefits and costs of different assumptions about likely regulation by other governmental entities, or the degree of compliance with the agency's own existing rules. In every case, an agency must measure both benefits and costs against the identical baseline. The agency should also provide an explanation of the plausibility of the alternative baselines used in the sensitivity analysis.

2. Evaluation of Alternatives. Agencies should identify alternatives that meet the criteria of the Executive Order as summarized at the beginning of this document, as well as identifying statutory requirements that affect the selection of a regulatory approach. To the fullest extent possible, benefits and costs should be expressed in discounted constant dollars.

Information on distributional impacts related to the alternatives should accompany the analysis of aggregate benefits and costs. Where relevant and feasible, agencies can also indicate how aggregate benefits and costs depend on the incidence of benefits and costs. Agencies should present a reasoned explanation or analysis to justify their choice among alternatives.

Where monetization is not possible for certain elements of the benefits or costs that are essential to consider, other quantitative and qualitative characterizations of these elements should be provided (see Sections 7 and 8 below). Cost-effectiveness analysis also should be used where possible to evaluate alternatives. Costs should be calculated net of monetized benefits. Where some benefits are monetizable and others are not, a cost-effectiveness analysis will generally not yield an unambiguous choice; nevertheless, such an analysis is helpful for calculating a "breakeven" value for the unmonetized benefits (i.e., a value that would result in the action having positive net benefits). Such a value can be evaluated for its reasonableness in the discussion of the justification of the proposed action. Cost-effectiveness analysis should also be used to compare regulatory alternatives in cases where the level of benefits is specified by statute.

If the proposed regulation is composed of a number of distinct provisions, it is important to evaluate the benefits and costs of the different provisions separately. The interaction effects between separate provisions (such that the existence of one provision affects the benefits or costs arising from another provision) may complicate the analysis but does not eliminate the need to examine provisions separately. In such a case, the desirability of a specific provision may be appraised by determining the net benefits of the proposed regulation with and without the provision in question. Where the number of provisions is large and interaction effects are pervasive, it is obviously impractical to analyze all possible combinations of provisions in this way. Some judgment must be used to select the most significant or suspect provisions for such analysis.

3. Discounting. One of the problems that arises in developing a benefit-cost analysis is that the benefits and costs often occur in different time periods. When this occurs, it is not appropriate, when comparing benefits and costs, to simply add up the benefits and costs accruing over time. Discounting takes account of the fact that resources (goods or services) that are available in a given year are worth more than the identical resources available in a later year. One reason for this is that resources can be invested so as to return more resources later.

(a) Basic considerations. Constant-dollar benefits and costs must be discounted to present values before benefits and costs in different years can be added together to determine overall net benefits. To obtain constant dollar estimates, benefit and cost streams in nominal dollars should be adjusted to correct for inflation. In assessing the present value of benefits and costs from a regulation, it may be necessary to consider implications of changing relative prices over time. In particular, the discount rate should not be adjusted for expected changes in the relative prices of goods over time. Instead, any changes in relative prices that are anticipated should be incorporated directly in the calculations of benefit and cost streams.

(b) Additional considerations. Modern research in economic theory has established a preferred model for discounting, sometimes referred to as the shadow price approach. The basic concept is that economic welfare is ultimately determined by consumption; investment affects welfare only to the extent that it affects current and future consumption. Thus, any effect that a government program has on public or private investment must be converted to an associated stream of effects on consumption before being discounted.

Converting investment-related benefits and costs to their consumption-equivalents · as required by this approach involves calculating the "shadow price of capital." This shadow price reflects the present value of the future changes in consumption arising from a marginal change in investment, using the consumption rate of interest (also termed the rate of time preference) as the discount rate. The calculation of the shadow price of capital requires assumptions about the extent to which government actions—including regulations—crowd out private investment, the social (i.e., before-tax) returns to this investment, and the rate of reinvestment of future yields from current investment.

4. Treatment of Risk and Uncertainty. The effects of regulatory actions frequently are not known with certainty but can be predicted in terms of their probability of occurrence. The term "risk" in this document refers generally to a probability distribution over a set of outcomes. When the outcomes in question are hazards or injuries, risk can be understood to refer to the probabilities of different potential severities of hazard or injury. For example, the risk of cancer from exposure to a chemical means a change in the probability of contracting cancer caused by that exposure. There also are risks associated with economic benefits and costs, e.g., the risk of a financial loss of $X means the probability of losing $X.

Often risks, benefits, and costs are measured imperfectly because key parameters are not known precisely; instead, the economic analysis must rely upon statistical probability distributions for the values of parameters. Both the inherent lack of certainty about the consequences of a potential hazard (for example, the odds of contracting cancer) and the lack of complete knowledge about parameter values that define risk relationships (for example, the relationship between presence of a carcinogen in the food supply and the rate of absorption of the carcinogen) should be considered.

Estimating the benefits and costs of risk-reducing regulations includes two components: a risk assessment that, in part, characterizes the probabilities of occurrence of outcomes of interest; and a valuation of the levels and changes in risk experienced by affected populations as a result of the regulation. It is essential that both parts of such evaluations be conceptually consistent. In particular, risk assessments should be conducted in a way that permits their use in a more general benefit-cost framework, just as the benefit-cost analysis should attempt to capture the results of the risk assessment and not oversimplify the results (e.g., the analysis should address the benefit and cost implications of probability distributions).

(a) Risk assessment. The assessment of outcomes associated with regulatory action to address risks to health, safety, and the environment raises a number of scientific difficulties. Key issues involve the quality and reliability of the data, models, assumptions, scientific inferences, and other information used in risk analyses. Analysts rarely, if ever, have complete information. It may be difficult to identify the full range of impacts. Little definitive may be known about the structure of key relationships and therefore about appropriate model specification. Data relating to effects that can be identified may be sketchy, incomplete, or subject to measurement error or statistical bias. Exposures and sensitivities to risks may vary considerably across the affected population. These difficulties can lead, for example, to a range of quantitative estimates of risk in health and ecological risk assessments that can span several orders of magnitude. Uncertainties in cost estimates also can be significant, in particular because of lack of experience with the adjustments that markets can make to reduce regulatory burdens, the difficulty of identifying and quantifying opportunity cost, and the potential for enhanced or retarded technical innovation. All of these concerns should be reflected in the uncertainties about outcomes that should be incorporated in the analysis.

The treatment of uncertainty in developing risk, benefit, and cost information also must be guided by the principles of full disclosure and transparency, as with other elements of an EA. Data, models, and their implications for risk assessment should be identified in the risk characterization. Inferences and assumptions should be identified and evaluated explicitly, together with adequate justifications of choices made, and assessments of the effects of these choices on the analysis.

Overall uncertainty is typically a consequence of uncertainties about many different factors. Appropriate statistical techniques should be used to combine uncertainties about separate factors into an overall probability distribution for a risk. When such techniques cannot be used, other methods may be useful for providing more complete information:

- Monte Carlo analysis and other simulation methods can be used to estimate probability distributions of the net benefits of alternative policy choices. It requires explicit quantitative characterization of variability to derive an overall probability distribution of net benefits.
- Sensitivity analysis is carried out by conducting analyses over the full range of plausible values of key parameters and plausible model specifications. Sensitivity analysis is particularly attractive when there are several easily identifiable critical assumptions in the analysis, when information is inadequate to carry out a more formal probabilistic simulation, or when the nature and scope of the regulation do not warrant more extensive analysis.
- Delphi methods involve derivation of estimates by groups of experts and can be used to identify attributes of subjective probability distributions. This method can be especially useful when there is diffuse or divergent prior knowledge. Care must be taken, however, to preserve any scientific controversy arising in a delphi analysis.
- Meta-analysis involves combining data or results from a number of different studies. For example, one could re-estimate key model parameters using combined data from a number of different sources, thereby improving confidence in the parameter estimates.

5. Assumptions. Where benefit or cost estimates are heavily dependent on certain assumptions, it is essential to make those assumptions explicit and, where alternative assumptions are plausible, to carry out sensitivity analyses based on the alternative assumptions. Because the adoption of a particular estimation methodology sometimes implies major hidden assumptions, it is important to analyze estimation methodologies carefully to make hidden assumptions explicit.

6. International Trade Effects. In calculating the benefits and costs of a proposed regulatory action, generally no explicit distinction needs to be made between domestic and foreign resources. Nonetheless, an awareness of the role of

international trade may be quite useful for assessing the benefits and costs of a proposed regulatory action. For example, the existence of foreign competition may make the demand curve facing a domestic industry more elastic than it would be otherwise. Elasticities of demand and supply frequently can significantly affect the magnitude of the benefits or costs of a regulation.

Regulations limiting imports—whether through direct prohibitions or fees, or indirectly through an adverse differential effect on foreign producers or consumers relative to domestic producers and consumers—raise special analytic issues. The economic loss to the United States from limiting imports should be reflected in the net benefit estimate. However, a benefit-cost analysis will generally not be able to measure the potential U.S. loss from the threat of future retaliation by foreign governments. This threat should then be treated as a qualitative cost (see Section 7).

7. Nonmonetized Benefits and Costs. Presentation of monetized benefits and costs is preferred where acceptable estimates are possible. However, monetization of some of the effects of regulations is often difficult if not impossible, and even the quantification of some effects may not be easy. Effects that cannot be fully monetized or otherwise quantified should be described. Those effects that can be quantified should be presented along with qualitative information to characterize effects that are not quantified.

8. Distributional Effects and Equity. Those who bear the costs of a regulation and those who enjoy its benefits often are not the same people. The term "distributional effects" refers to the description of the net effects of a regulatory alternative across the population and economy, divided up in various ways (e.g., income groups, race, sex, industrial sector). Benefits and costs of a regulation may be distributed unevenly over time, perhaps spanning several generations. Distributional effects may also arise through "transfer payments" arising from a regulatory action. For example, the revenue collected through a fee, surcharge, or tax (in excess of the cost of any service provided) is a transfer payments.

Where distributive effects are thought to be important, the effects of various regulatory alternatives should be described quantitatively to the extent possible, including their magnitude, likelihood, and incidence of effects on particular groups. Agencies should be alert for situations in which regulatory alternatives result in significant changes in treatment or outcomes for different groups. Effects on the distribution of income that are transmitted through changes in market prices can be important, albeit sometimes difficult to assess. The EA should also present information on the streams of benefits and costs over time in order to provide a basis for judging intertemporal distributional consequences, particularly where intergenerational effects are concerned.

B. Benefit Estimates

The EA should state the beneficial effects of the proposed regulatory change and its principal alternatives. In each case, there should be an explanation of the mechanism by which the proposed action is expected to yield the anticipated benefits. An attempt should be made to quantify all potential real incremental benefits to society in monetary terms to the maximum extent possible. A schedule of monetized benefits should be included that would show the type of benefit and when it would accrue; the numbers in this table should be expressed in constant, undiscounted dollars. Any benefits that cannot be monetized, such as an increase in the rate of introducing more productive new technology or a decrease in the risk of extinction of endangered species, should also be presented and explained.

The EA should identify and explain the data or studies on which benefit estimates are based with enough detail to permit independent assessment and verification of the results. Where benefit estimates are derived from a statistical study, the EA should provide sufficient information so that an independent observer can determine the representativeness of the sample, the reliability of extrapolations used to develop aggregate estimates, and the statistical significance of the results.

The calculation of benefits (including benefits of risk reductions) should reflect the full probability distribution of potential consequences. For example, extreme safety or health results should be weighted, along with other possible outcomes, by estimates of their probability of occurrence based on the available evidence to estimate the expected result of a proposed regulation. To the extent possible, the probability distributions of benefits should be presented. If fundamental scientific disagreement or lack of knowledge precludes construction of a scientifically defensible probability distribution, benefits should be described under plausible alternative assumptions, along with a characterization of the evidence underlying each alternative view. This will allow for a reasoned determination by decisionmakers of the appropriate level of regulatory action.

1.   General Considerations.   The concept of "opportunity cost" is the appropriate construct for valuing both benefits and costs.   The principle of "willingness-to-pay" captures the notion of opportunity cost by providing an aggregate measure of what individuals are willing to forgo to enjoy a particular benefit. Either willingness-to-pay (WTP) or willingness-to-accept (WTA) can provide an appropriate measure of benefits, depending on the allocation of property rights.   The common preference for WTP over WTA measures is based on the empirical difficulties in estimating the latter.

2. Principles for Valuing Benefits Directly Traded in Markets. Ordinarily, goods and services are to be valued at their market prices. However, in some instances, the market value of a good or service may not reflect its true value to society. If a regulatory alternative involves changes in such a good or service, its monetary value for purposes of benefit-cost analysis should be derived using an estimate of its true value to society (often called its "shadow price").

3. Principles for Valuing Benefits That Are Indirectly Traded in Markets. In some important instances, a benefit corresponds to a good or service that is indirectly traded in the marketplace. Examples include reductions in health-and-safety risks, the use-values of environmental amenities and scenic vistas. To

estimate the monetary value of such an indirectly traded good, the willingness-to-pay valuation methodology is considered the conceptually superior approach.

4. Principles and Methods for Valuing Goods That Are Not Traded Directly or Indirectly in Markets. Some types of goods, such as preserving environmental or cultural amenities apart from their use and direct enjoyment by people, are not traded directly or indirectly in markets. For many of these goods, particularly goods providing "nonuse" values, contingent-valuation methods may provide the only analytical approaches currently available for estimating values.

5. Methods for Valuing Health and Safety Benefits. Regulations that address health and safety concerns often yield a variety of benefits traded directly in markets, benefits indirectly traded in markets, and benefits not traded in markets. A major component of many such regulations is a reduction is the risk of illness, injury or premature death. There are differences of opinion about the various approaches for monetizing such risk reductions. In assessing health and safety benefits, the analysis should present estimates of both the risks of nonfatal illness or injury and fatality risks, and may include any particular strengths or weakness of such analyses the agencies think appropriate, in order to accurately assess the benefits of government action.

C. Cost Estimates

1. General Considerations. The preferred measure of cost is the "opportunity cost" of the resources used or the benefits forgone as a result of the regulatory action. Opportunity costs include, but are not limited to, private-sector compliance costs and government administrative costs. Opportunity costs also include losses in consumers' or producers' surpluses, discomfort or inconvenience, and loss of time. These effects should be incorporated in the analysis and given a monetary value wherever possible. (Producers' surplus is the difference between the amount a producer is paid for a unit of a good and the minimum amount the producer would accept to supply that unit. It is measured by the area between the price and the supply curve for that unit. Consumers' surplus is the difference between what a consumer pays for a unit of a good and the maximum amount the consumer would be willing to pay for that unit. It is measured by the distance between the price and the demand curve for that unit.)

The opportunity cost of an alternative also incorporates the value of the benefits forgone as a consequence of that alternative. For example, the opportunity cost of banning a product (e.g., a drug, food additive, or hazardous chemical) is the forgone net benefit of that product, taking into account the mitigating effects of potential substitutes.

All costs calculated should be incremental, that is, they should represent changes in costs that would occur if the regulatory option is chosen compared to costs in the base case (ordinarily no regulation or the existing regulation) or under a less stringent alternative.

2.   Real Costs Versus Transfer Payments.   An important, but sometimes difficult, problem in cost estimation is to distinguish between real costs and transfer payments.   Transfer payments are not social costs but rather are payments that reflect a redistribution of wealth.   While transfers should not be included in the EA's estimates of the benefits and costs of a regulation, they may be important for describing the distributional effects of a regulation.   Scarcity rents and monopoly profits, insurance payments, government subsidies and taxes, and distribution expenses are four potential problem areas that may affect both social benefits and costs as well as involve significant transfer payments.

Appendix D
Topical Bibliography of Studies on the Effects of Regulation

1. STUDIES ON A WIDE RANGE OF KINDS OF REGULATION, OR REGULATION IN GENERAL

Bord, Nancy A. and William G. Laffer III, "George Bush's Hidden Tax: The Explosion in Regulation," *Backgrounder* no. 905 (Washington, D.C.: The Heritage Foundation, July 10, 1992).

Hahn, Robert W. "Regulation: Past, Present and Future," *Harvard Journal of Law and Public Policy* 13, no. 1 (Winter 1990): 167–228.

Hahn, Robert W. and John A. Hird, "The Costs and Benefits of Regulation: Review and Synthesis," *Yale Journal on Regulation* 8, no. 1 (Winter 1991): 233–278.

Hahn, Robert W. and Thomas D. Hopkins, "Regulation/Deregulation: Looking Backward, Looking Forward," *The American Enterprise* 3, no. 4 (July/August 1992): 70–79.

Hanke, Steve H., and Stephen J. K. Walters, "Social Regulation: A Report Card. *Journal of Regulation and Social Costs* 1, no. 1 (September 1990): 5–34.

Hopkins, Thomas D. *Cost of Regulation*, Rochester, N.Y.: Rochester Institute of Technology Public Policy Working Paper, December 1991.

Hopkins, Thomas D. "The Costs of Federal Regulation," *Journal of Regulation and Social Costs* 2, no. 1 (March 1992): 5–31.

Litan, Robert E., and William D. Nordhaus, *Reforming Federal Regulation*. New Haven, Conn.: Yale University Press, 1983.

Warren, Melinda, and James Lis, *Regulatory Standstill: Analysis of the 1993 Federal Regulatory Budget*, Occasional Paper 105, St. Louis: Center for the Study of American Business, Washington University, Missouri, May 1992.

Weidenbaum, Murray L., and Robert DeFina, *The Cost of Federal Regulation of Economic Activity*. Washington, D.C.: American Enterprise Institute Reprint no. 88, May 1978.

Weidenbaum, Murray L. *The Future of Business Regulation: Private Action and Public Demand*. New York: AMACOM (a division of the American Management Association): 1979.

Weidenbaum, Murray L. *The New Wave of Business Regulation*, Contemporary Issues Series no. 40, St. Louis: Center for the Study of American Business, Washington University, May 1992.

2. **STUDIES ON PARTICULAR KINDS OF REGULATION (OTHER THAN REGULATION OF FIRMS' EMPLOYMENT POLICIES)**

American Bankers Association, *Survey of Regulatory Burden: Summary of Results*, Washington, D.C.: American Bankers Association, June 1992.

Baily, Martin Neil, "Research and Development Cost and Returns: The U.S. Pharmaceutical Industry," *Journal of Political Economy* (January/February 1972): 70–85.

Barnekov, C. "Trucking, U.S. Industrial Outlook," *Transportation Services* 52 (1989): 4, 6.

Barnekov, C., and A. Kleit, *The Costs of Railroad Regulation: A Further Analysis*. Washington, D.C.: Federal Trade Commission Working Paper No. 164, 1988.

Bartel, Ann P., and Lacy Glenn Thomas, "Direct and Indirect Effects of Regulation: A New Look at OSHA's Impact," *Journal of Law and Economics* 28, no. 1 (April 1985): 1–25.

Bartel, Ann P., and Lacy Glenn Thomas, "Predation Through Regulation: The Wage and Profit Effects of the Occupational Safety and Health Administration and the Environmental Protection Agency," *Journal of Law and Economics* 30, no. 2 (October 1987): 239–264.

Board of Governors of the Federal Reserve System, *Federal Reserve Bulletin* 78, no. 6 (June 1992): A23–A24, A38.

Board of Governors of the Federal Reserve System, "Aggregate Reserves of Depository Institutions and the Monetary Base." *Federal Reserve Statistical Release H.3 (502)* (June 18, 1992): Table 2.

Boyer, "The Costs of Price Regulation: Lessons from Railroad Deregulation," *Rand Journal of Economics* 18 (1987): 408.

Caves, Christensen, Tretheway, and Windle, "An Assessment of the Efficiency Effects of U.S. Airline Deregulation via an International Comparison," in *Public Regulation: New Perspectives on Institutions and Policies* edited by Elizabeth E. Bailey, Cambridge, Mass.: MIT Press, 1987.

Cowin, Andrew J. "How Washington Boosts State and Local Budget Deficits," *Backgrounder* no. 908, Washington, D.C.: The Heritage Foundation (July 31, 1992).

Crandall, Robert W. *Why Is the Cost of Environmental Regulation So High?*, Policy Study no. 110, Center for the Study of American Business, Washington University, St. Louis, Missouri, May 1992.

Crandall, Robert W. and John D. Graham, "The Effect of Fuel Economy Standards on Automobile Safety," *Journal of Law and Economics* XXXII (April 1989): 97–118.

Delaney, "Managerial and Financial Challenges Facing Transport Leaders," *Transportation Quarterly* 40 (1986): 29.

Denison, Edward F. *Trends in American Economic Growth, 1929–1982*. Washington, D.C.: Brookings Institution, 1985.

Economic Report of the President. Washington, D.C.: U.S. Government Printing Office, February 1992, Tables B–1, B–3 and B–56, pp. 298, 302 and 361.

Evans, D. "The Differential Effects of Regulation across Plant Size: Comment on Pashigian." *Journal of Law and Economics* 29, no. 1 (April 1986): 187–200.

Genetski, Robert, "The True Cost of Government," *The Wall Street Journal* (February 19, 1992): A15.

Grabowski, Henry G. *Drug Regulation and Innovation*. Washington, D.C.: American Enterprise Institute, 1976.

Gray, Wayne B. "The Cost of Regulation: OSHA, EPA and the Productivity Slowdown," *American Economic Review* 77, no. 5 (December 1987): 998–1006.

Gray, Wayne B. "The Impact of OSHA and EPA Regulation on Productivity Growth," *Journal of Regulation and Social Costs* 1, no. 3 (June 1991): 25–47.

Hanke, Steve H. and Stephen J.K. Walters, "Social Regulation: A Report Card," *Journal of Regulation and Social Costs* 1, no. 1 (September 1990): 5–34.

Hazilla, Michael and Raymond J. Kopp, "Social Cost of Environmental Quality Regulations: A General Equilibrium Analysis," *Journal of Political Economy* 98, no. 4 (1990): 853–873.

Huber, Peter W. "Exorcists vs. Gatekeepers in Risk Regulation," *Regulation* (November/December 1983): 23–32.

Huber, Peter W. "Biotechnology and the Regulation Hydra," *Technology Review* 90, no. 8 (November/December 1987): 57–65.

Jorgenson, Dale W., and David T. Slesnick, "Efficiency Versus Equity in Natural Gas Price Regulation," *Journal of Econometrics* 30 (1985): 301–316.

Jorgenson, Dale W. and Daniel T. Slesnick, "General Equilibrium Analysis of Natural Gas Price Regulation," in *Public Regulation: New Perspectives on Institutions and Policies* edited by Elizabeth E. Bailey. Cambridge, Mass.: MIT Press, 1987.

Jorgenson, Dale W., and Peter J. Wilcoxen, "Environmental Regulation and U.S. Economic Growth," Harvard Institute of Economic Research Discussion Paper no. 1458, October 1989.

Jorgenson, Dale W., and Peter J. Wilcoxen, "Environmental Regulation and U.S. Economic Growth." *Rand Journal of Economics*, 21, no. 2 (Summer 1990a): 314–340.

Joskow, Paul L. "Expanding Competitive Opportunities in Electricity Generation," *Regulation* 15, no. 1 (Winter 1992): 25–37.

Kazman, Sam, "Deadly Overcaution: FDA's Drug Approval Process," *Journal of Regulation and Social Costs* 1, no. 1 (September 1990): 35–54.

Miles, Marc A. *Beyond Monetarism: Finding the Road to Stable Money.* New York: Basic Books, 1984, 111–36, 158–80 (discussing effects of banking regulation on competition between banks and money market funds, and between domestic and foreign banks).

Mitchell, Mark L., and J. Harold Mulherin, "Finessing the Political System: The Cigarette Advertising Ban," *Southern Economic Journal* (April 1988): 855–62.

Moore, "The Beneficiaries of Trucking Deregulation," *Journal of Law and Economics* 21 (1978): 327, 342.

Morrison, Steve, and Clifford Winston, *The Economic Effects of Airline Deregulation.* Washington, D.C.: Brookings Institution, 1986.

Office of Management and Budget, *Information Resources Management Plan of the Federal Government.* Washington, D.C.: U.S. Government Printing Office, November 1991, pp. II–3 to II–8 ("The Fiscal Year 1991 Information Collection Budget").

Office of Management and Budget, *Budget of the United States Government, Fiscal Year 1993. Washington*, D.C.: U.S. Government Printing Office, January 1992, Part One, Table 17–3, pp. 402–06.

Office of Management and Budget, *Budget of the United States Government, Fiscal Year 1993, Supplement.* Washington, D.C.: U.S. Government Printing Office, February 1992, Part Five, Tables 2.1 and 2.5, pp. 21–22, 34–35.

Owen, D. *Deregulation in the Trucking Industry.* Washington, D.C.: Federal Trade Commission, 1988.

Pashigian, B. Peter, "The Effects of Regulation on Optimal Plant Size and Factor Shares," *Journal of Law and Economics* 27, no. 1 (April 1984): 1–28.

Pashigian, B. Peter, "Environmental Regulation: Whose Self Interests Are Being Protected?" *Economic Inquiry* 23, no. 4 (October 1985): 551–84.

Pashigian, B. Peter, "Reply to Evans," *Journal of Law and Economics* 29, no. (April 1986): 201–09.

Peltzman, Sam, "An Evaluation of Consumer Protection Legislation: The 1962 Drug Amendments," *Journal of Political Economy* (September 1973): 1049–1091.

Portney, Paul R. "Economics and the Clean Air Act," *Journal of Economic Perspectives* 4, no. 4 (Fall 1990): 173–81.

Rubin, Paul H. "Regulatory Relief or Power Grab: Should Congress Expand FDA's Enforcement Authority?" *Backgrounder* no. 900 (Washington, D.C.: The Heritage Foundation, June 11, 1992).

Tubbs, Alan R. "Statement on Behalf of the American Bankers Association Before the Federal Financial Institutions Examination Council," Kansas City, Mo. June 18, 1992 (available from the American Bankers Association in Washington, D.C.).

Yandle, Bruce, *Why Environmentalists Should Be Efficiency Lovers*, Formal
    Publication no. 105, St. Louis: Center for the Study of American Business,
    Washington University, April 1991.
Wardell, William, "More Regulation or Better Therapies?" *Regulation*
    (September/October 1979): 25–33.
Weidenbaum, Murray L. *The New Wave of Business Regulation*, Contemporary
    Issues Series no. 40, St. Louis: Center for the Study of American Business,
    Washington University, May 1992.
Winston, Clifford, "Conceptual Developments in the Economics of Transportation:
    An Interpretive Survey," Journal of Economic Literature 23 (1985): 57, 84.

3. STUDIES ON THE REGULATION OF COMPENSATION AND HOURS OF WORK

Allen, Steven, "Much Ado about Davis-Bacon: A Critical Review and New
    Evidence," *Journal of Law and Economics* 26 (October 1983): 707–36.
Bonilla, Carlos, *Higher Wages, Greater Poverty: Trapping Americans in Poverty*.
    Washington, D.C.: Employment Policies Institute, April 1992.
Brown, Charles, Curtis Gilroy, and Andrew Kohen, "The Effect of the Minimum
    Wage on Employment and Unemployment," *Journal of Economic Literature*
    22 (June 1982): 487–528.
Darby, Michael, "A Long-Run Analysis of Minimum Wage Laws," University
    of California at Los Angeles Economics Department Discussion Paper no. 68,
    November 1979.
Falconer, Robert T. "The minimum wage: a perspective," *Federal Reserve Bank
    of New York Quarterly Review* (Autumn 1978): 3–6.
Goldfarb, Robert, and John Morrall III, "The Davis-Bacon Act: An Appraisal of
    Recent Studies," *Industrial and Labor Relations Review* 34 (January 1981):
    191–207.
Hamermesh, Daniel S. "Minimum Wages and the Demand for Labor," *Economic
    Inquiry* 20 (July 1982): 365–80.
Hamermesh, Daniel S. "The Demand for Labor in the Long Run," in *Handbook
    of Labor Economics*, Vol. 1, edited by Orley C. Ashenfelter and Richard
    Layard, 429–72. Amsterdam: North-Holland Publishing Company, 1986.
Linneman, Peter, "The Economic Impacts of Minimum Wage Laws: A New
    Look at an Old Question," *Journal of Political Economy* 90, no. 3 (June 1982):
    443–69.
Meyer, Robert H., and David A. Wise, "The Effects of the Minimum Wage on
    the Employment and Earnings of Youth," *Journal of Labor Economics* 1
    (1983): 66–100.
Mincer, Jacob, "Unemployment Effects of Minimum Wages," *Journal of Political
    Economy* 84 (August 1976): S87–S104.
Minimum Wage Study Commission, *Report of the Minimum Wage Study
    Commission*, Washington, D.C.: 1981.

Neumark, David, "Employment Effects of Minimum and Subminimum Wages," Washington, D.C.: Employment Policies Institute, February 1993.

Ragan, James F., Jr. "Minimum Wages and the Youth Labor Market," *Review of Economics and Statistics* 59 (May 1977): 129–36.

Ragan, James F., Jr. "Minimum Wage Legislation: Goals and Realities," *Nebraska Journal of Economics and Business* 17 (Autumn 1978): 21–28.

Rottenberg, Simon, ed. *The Economics of Legal Minimum Wages.* Washington, D.C.: American Enterprise Institute, 1981.

Stigler, George J. "The Economics of Minimum Wage Legislation," *American Economic Review* 36 (June 1946): 358–67.

Taylor, Lowell J. "The Employment Effects in Retail Trade of a Minimum Wage, Evidence from California," Washington, D.C.: Employment Policies Institute, June 1993.

Vandenbrink, Donna C. "The Minimum Wage: No Minor Matter for Teens," *FRB Chicago Economic Perspectives* (March/April 1987): 19–28.

Welch, Finis, "Minimum Wage Legislation in the United States," *Economic Inquiry* 12 (September 1974): 285–318.

Welch, Finis, *Minimum Wages: Issues and Evidence* (Washington, D.C.: American Enterprise Institute, 1978).

4.   STUDIES ON THE REGULATION OF MANDATED BENEFITS

Bellante, Don and Philip K. Porter, "A Subjectivist Economic Analysis of Government-Mandated Employee Benefits," *Harvard Journal of Law and Public Policy* 13, no. 2 (Spring 1990): 657–87.

Bord, Nancy A. and William G. Laffer III, "George Bush's Hidden Tax: The Explosion in Regulation," *Backgrounder* no. 905 (Washington, D.C.: The Heritage Foundation, July 10, 1992): 8–9 (discussing the Americans with Disabilities Act).

Ehrenberg, Ronald G. and Robert S. Smith, "The Structure of Compensation" in *Modern Labor Economics: Theory and Public Policy,* 4th ed. (New York: HarperCollins, 1991).

Epstein, Richard A. *Forbidden Grounds: The Case Against Employment Discrimination Laws.* Cambridge, Mass.: Harvard University Press, 1992. (especially Chapter 22, "Disability Discrimination," pp. 480–94).

O'Neill, June E. and David M. O'Neill, "The Impact of a Health Insurance mandate on Labor Costs and Employment, Empirical Evidence," Washington, D.C.: Employment Policies Institute, September 1993.

O'Quinn, Robert P. "The Americans with Disabilities Act: Time for Amendments" Cato Institute, *Policy Analysis,* no. 158 (August 9, 1991).

5. STUDIES ON THE REGULATION OF INDUSTRIAL RELATIONS

Addison, John T., and Barry T. Hirsch, *The Economic Analysis of Unions: New Approaches and Evidence*. Boston: Allen and Unwin, 1986 (especially chapters 4, "Unions, Bargaining, and Strikes", and 5, "Union Effects on Relative Wages").

Addison, John T., and Barry T. Hirsch, "Union Effects on Productivity, Profits, and Growth: Has the Long Run Arrived?" *Journal of Labor Economics* 7 (January 1989): 72–105.

Ashenfelter, Orley C., and James Brown, "Testing the Efficiency of Employment Contracts," *Journal of Political Economy* 94, no. 3, Part 2 (June 1986): S40–S87.

Ashenfelter, Orley C., and George Johnson, "Bargaining Theory, Trade Unions, and Industrial Strike Activity," *American Economic Review* 59 (March 1969): 35–49.

Brown, Charles, and James L. Medoff, "Trade Unions in the Production Process," *Journal of Political Economy* 86 (June 1978): 355–78.

Clark, Kim B., "Unionization and Firm Performance: The Impact on Profits, Growth, and Productivity," *American Economic Review* (December 1984).

Ehrenberg, Ronald G. and Robert S. Smith, "Unions and Collective Bargaining in the Private Sector" in *Modern Labor Economics: Theory and Public Policy*, 4th ed. New York: HarperCollins, 1991.

Farber, Henry S., "The Analysis of Union Behavior," in *Handbook of Labor Economics*, Vol. 2 edited by Orley C. Ashenfelter and Richard Layard. Amsterdam: North-Holland Publishing Company, 1986.

Freeman, Richard B., and James L. Medoff, "The Two Faces of Unionism," *Public Interest* no. 57 (Fall 1979): 69–93.

Freeman, Richard B., and James L. Medoff, *What Do Unions Do?* New York: Basic Books, 1984.

Kennan, John, "The Economics of Strikes," in *Handbook of Labor Economics*, Vol. 2 edited by Orley C. Ashenfelter and Richard Layard. Amsterdam: North-Holland Publishing Company, 1986.

Lewis, H. Gregg, *Union Relative Wage Effects: A Survey*. Chicago: University of Chicago Press, 1986.

Linneman, Peter, Michael Wachter, and W. Carter, "Evaluating the Evidence on Union Employment and Wages," *Industrial and Labor Relations Review* (October 1990).

Reynolds, Morgan O. "Trade Unions in the Production Process Reconsidered," *Journal of Political Economy* 4 94 (1986).

6.   STUDIES ON THE REGULATION OF EMPLOYMENT DISCRIMINATION

Ashenfelter, Orley C., and James J. Heckman, "Measuring the Effects of an Antidiscrimination Program," in *Evaluating the Labor-Market Effects of Social Programs* edited by Orley C. Ashenfelter and James Blum, 46–84. Princeton, N.J.: Industrial Relations Section, Princeton University, 1976.

Bord, Nancy A. and William G. Laffer III, "George Bush's Hidden Tax: The Explosion in Regulation," *Backgrounder* no. 905 (Washington, D.C.: The Heritage Foundation, July 10, 1992), 4, 9–10 (discussing Title VII of the Civil Rights Act of 1964, as amended by the Civil Rights Act of 1991).

Brown, Charles, "The Federal Attack on Labor Market Discrimination: The Mouse That Roared?" Washington, D.C.: National Bureau of Economic Research Working Paper 1981.

Donohue, John J. "Is Title VII Efficient?" *University of Pennsylvania Law Review* 134 (1986): 1411.

Donohue, John J. "Further Thoughts on Employment Discrimination Legislation: A Reply to Judge Posner," *University of Pennsylvania Law Review* 136 (1987): 523.

Donohue, John J. "Advocacy versus Analysis in Assessing Employment Discrimination Law: A Review of Richard Epstein's Forbidden Grounds," *Stanford Law Review* (1992).

Donohue, John J., and James J. Heckman, "Continuous Versus Episodic Change: The Impact of Civil Rights Policy on the Economic Status of Blacks," *Journal of Economic Literature* 29 (1991).

Epstein, Richard A. "The Paradox of Civil Rights," *Yale Law and Policy Review* 8 (1990): 299–323.

Epstein, Richard A. *Forbidden Grounds: The Case Against Employment Discrimination Laws*. Cambridge, Mass.: Harvard University Press, 1992.

Freeman, Richard B. "Changes in the Labor Market for Black Americans, 1948–1972," *Brookings Papers on Economic Activity* (1973): 67–131.

Freeman, Richard B. "Black Economic Progress after 1964: Who Has Gained and Why?" in *Studies in Labor Markets* edited by Sherwin Rosen, 247–94. Chicago: University of Chicago Press, 1981.

Heckman, James J. "The Impact of Government on the Economic Status of Black Americans," in *The Question of Discrimination: Racial Inequality in the U.S. Labor Market*. 1989.

Heckman, James J., and Brook S. Payner, "Determining the Impact of Federal Antidiscrimination Policy on the Economic Status of Blacks: A Study of South Carolina," *American Economic Review* 79 (1989).

Heckman, James J., and J. Hoult Verkerke, "Racial Disparity and Employment Discrimination Law: An Economic Perspective," *Yale Law and Policy Review* 8 (1990): 276–98.

Heckman, James J., and J. Hoult Verkerke, "Response to Epstein," *Yale Law and Policy Review* 8 (1990): 324–26.

Leonard, Jonathan S. "Antidiscrimination or Reverse Discrimination: The Impact of Changing Demographics, Title VII, and Affirmative Action on Productivity," *Journal of Human Resources* XIX, no. 2 (Spring 1984): 145–74.

Leonard, Jonathan S. "The Effectiveness of Equal Employment Law and Affirmative Action Regulation," in *Research in Labor Economics* Volume 8, Part B edited by Ronald G. Ehrenberg. Greenwich, Conn.: JAI Press, 1986.

O'Quinn, Robert P. "The Americans with Disabilities Act: Time for Amendments," Cato Institute *Policy Analysis* no. 158 (August 9, 1991).

Posner, Richard A. "The Efficiency and Efficacy of Title VII," *University of Pennsylvania Law Review* 136 (1987): 513–22.

Smith, James P., and Finis R. Welch, "Affirmative Action and Labor Markets," *Journal of Labor Economics* 2 (1984).

Smith, James P., and Finis R. Welch, "Black Economic Progress after Myrdal," *Journal of Economic Literature* 27 (June 1989): 519–64.

7. STUDIES ON THE REGULATION OF OCCUPATIONAL SAFETY AND HEALTH

Bartel, Ann P., and Lacy Glenn Thomas, "Direct and Indirect Effects of Regulation: A New Look at OSHA's Impact," *Journal of Law and Economics* 28, no. 1 (April 1985): 1–25.

Bartel, Ann P., and Lacy Glenn Thomas, "Predation Through Regulation: The Wage and Profit Effects of the Occupational Safety and Health Administration and the Environmental Protection Agency," *Journal of Law and Economics* 30, no. 2 (October 1987): 239–64.

Ehrenberg, Ronald G., and Robert S. Smith, "Compensating Wage Differentials in Labor Markets" in *Modern Labor Economics: Theory and Public Policy,* 4th ed. New York: HarperCollins, 1991.

Gray, Wayne B. "The Cost of Regulation: OSHA, EPA and the Productivity Slowdown," *American Economic Review* 77, no. 5 (December 1987): 998–1006.

Gray, Wayne B. "The Impact of OSHA and EPA Regulation on Productivity Growth," *Journal of Regulation and Social Costs* 1, no. 3 (June 1991): 25–47.

8. SOURCES ON GENERAL EQUILIBRIUM ANALYSIS, AND ON THE APPLICATION OF GENERAL EQUILIBRIUM MODELS TO TAXATION AND REGULATION

A. General Background Sources

Bergman, Lars, Dale W. Jorgenson, and Erno Zalai, eds. *General Equilibrium Modeling and Economic Policy Analysis*. Cambridge, Mass.: B. Blackwell, 1990.

Hicks, John R. *Value and Capital: An Inquiry into Some Fundamental Principles of Economic Theory*, 2d ed. Oxford: Clarendon Press, 1939, pp. 1–111.

Johnson, Harry G., *The Two-Sector Model of General Equilibrium*. London: Allen and Unwin, 1971.

Jorgenson, Dale W., and Daniel T. Slesnick, "General Equilibrium Analysis of Economic Policy," in *New Developments in Applied General Equilibrium Analysis* edited by John Piggott and John Whalley, 293–370. Cambridge: Cambridge University Press, 1985.

Scarf, Herbert E. and John B. Shoven, *Applied General Equilibrium Analysis*. New York: Cambridge University Press, 1984.

B. General Theoretical Models of the Effects of Taxation and Regulation

Canto, Victor A., "Taxation in a Closed Economy Intertemporal Model with a Variable Supply of Labor to the Market Sector," in *Foundations of Supply-Side Economics: Theory and Evidence* edited by Victor A. Canto, Douglas H. Joines and Arthur B. Laffer, 25–44. New York: Academic Press, 1983.

Canto, Victor A., Douglas H. Joines, and Arthur B. Laffer, "Tax Rates, Factor Employment, Market Production, and Welfare," in *Foundations of Supply-Side Economics: Theory and Evidence* edited by Victor A. Canto, Douglas H. Joines, and Arthur B. Laffer, New York: Academic Press, 1983.

Evans, Paul, "Fiscal Policy and the Labor Market," in *Foundations of Supply-Side Economics: Theory and Evidence* edited by Victor A. Canto, Douglas H. Joines, and Arthur B. Laffer, New York: Academic Press, 1983.

Harberger, Arnold C. *Taxation and Welfare*. Chicago: University of Chicago Press, 1974.

Joines, Douglas H. "A Neoclassical Model of Fiscal Policy, Employment, and Capital Accumulation," in *Foundations of Supply-Side Economics: Theory and Evidence* edited by Victor A. Canto, Douglas H. Joines, and Arthur B. Laffer, New York: Academic Press, 1983.

Laffer, Arthur B. "Supply-Side Economics," *Financial Analysts Journal* (September/October 1981): 29–43.

Miles, Marc A. *Beyond Monetarism: Finding the Road to Stable Money*. New York: Basic Books, 1984, pp. 120–124 (explaining how regulation can be equivalent to a tax on the activity it governs, insofar as it increases the implicit "wedge" between the gross price incurred by firms or their customers and the net return received by labor and capital).

C. Quantitative Models of the Entire Economy, as Applied to Taxation

Auerbach, Alan J., Laurence J. Kotlikoff, and Jonathan Skinner, "The Efficiency Gains from Dynamic Tax Reform," *International Economic Review* 24, no. 1 (February 1983): 81–100.

Auerbach, Alan J., and Laurence J. Kotlikoff, *Dynamic Fiscal Policy*. New York: Cambridge University Press, 1987).

Ballard, Charles L., Don Fullerton, John B. Shoven, and John Whalley, *A General Equilibrium Model for Tax Policy Evaluation*. Chicago: University of Chicago Press, 1985.

Ballard, Charles L., John B. Shoven, and John Whalley, "General Equilibrium Computations of the Marginal Welfare Costs of Taxes in the United States," *American Economic Review* 75, No. 1, (March 1985): 128–138.

Ballard, Charles L., John B. Shoven, and John Whalley, "The Total Welfare Cost of the United States Tax System: A General Equilibrium Approach," *National Tax Journal* XXXVIII, no. 2 (June 1985): 125–140.

Fullerton, Don, Yolanda K. Henderson, and John B. Shoven, "A Comparison of Methodologies in Empirical General Equilibrium Models of Taxation," in *Applied General Equilibrium Analysis* edited by Herbert E. Scarf and John B. Shoven, 367–410. New York: Cambridge University Press, 1984.

Goulder, Lawrence H., John B. Shoven, and John Whalley, "Domestic Tax Policy and the Foreign Sector: The Importance of Alternative Foreign Sector Formulations to Results from a General Equilibrium Tax Analysis Model," in *Behavioral Simulation Methods in Tax Policy Analysis* edited by Martin S. Feldstein, 333–364. Chicago: University of Chicago Press, 1983.

Jorgenson, Dale W., and Kun-Young Yun, "Tax Reform and U.S. Economic Growth," *Journal of Political Economy* 98, no. 5, Part 2 (1990): S151–S193.

Jorgenson, Dale W., and Kun-Young Yun, *Tax Reform and the Cost of Capital*. Oxford: Clarendon Press, 1991.

Kimbell, Larry J. and Glenn W. Harrison, "General Equilibrium Analysis of Regional Fiscal Incidence," in *Applied General Equilibrium Analysis* edited by Herbert E. Scarf, and John B. Shoven, 275–313. New York: Cambridge University Press, 1984.

Piggott, John, and John Whalley, *UK Tax Policy and Applied General Equilibrium Analysis*. New York: Cambridge University Press, 1985.

Shoven, John B., and John Whalley, "A General Equilibrium Calculation of the Effects of Differential Taxation of Income from Capital in the U.S.," *Journal of Public Economics* 1 (1972):281–321.

D.   Studies Applying Quantitative General Equilibrium Models to Regulation

Hazilla, Michael and Raymond J. Kopp, "Social Cost of Environmental Quality Regulations: A General Equilibrium Analysis," *Journal of Political Economy* 98, no. 4 (1990): 853–873.

Jorgenson, Dale W., and David T. Slesnick, "Efficiency Versus Equity in Natural Gas Price Regulation," *Journal of Econometrics* 30 (1985): 301–316.

Jorgenson, Dale W., and Daniel T. Slesnick, "General Equilibrium Analysis of Natural Gas Price Regulation," in *Public Regulation: New Perspectives on Institutions and Policies* edited by Elizabeth E. Bailey, 153–90. Cambridge, Mass.: MIT Press, 1987.

Jorgenson, Dale W., and Peter J. Wilcoxen, "Environmental Regulation and U.S. Economic Growth," *Harvard Institute of Economic Research* Discussion Paper no. 1458, (October 1989).

Jorgenson, Dale W., and Peter J. Wilcoxen, "Environmental Regulation and U.S. Economic Growth." *Rand Journal of Economics*, 21(2) (Summer 1990): 314–340.

Bibliography

Addison, John T., and Barry T. Hirsch, "Union Effects on Productivity, Profits, and Growth: Has the Long Run Arrived?" *Journal of Labor Economics* 7 (January 1989): 72–105.

Administrative Conference of the United States, *A Guide to Federal Agency Rulemaking.* Washington, D.C.: Administrative Conference of the United States, 1991.

Advisory Commission on Intergovernmental Relations, "Perspectives on Regulatory Federalism," *Intergovernmental Perspectives,* 18, no. 4 (Fall 1992).

"America's Parasite Economy," *The Economist,* (October 10, 1992).

Anderson, Gary, and Lowell Gallaway, "Derailing the Small Business Job Express," Washington, D.C.: Joint Economic Committee of the U.S. Congress, November, 1992, pp. 21–24.

Anthony, Robert A. "Which Agency Interpretations Should Bind Citizens and Courts?" *Yale Journal on Regulation* 7, no. 1 (Winter 1990): 1–64.

Atkinson, Anthony, and Joseph Stiglitz, *Public Economics.* New York: McGraw Hill, 1980.

Auchter, Thorne, *Toward Common Measures.* Washington, D.C.: Federal Focus, Inc. and the Institute for Regulatory Policy, 1991.

Auchter, Thorne, "The President's Next Step in Regulatory Reform," *Journal of Regulation and Social Costs* 1, no. 4 (November 1991): 3–62.

Ballard, Charles L., Don Fullerton, John B. Shoven, and John Whalley, *A General Equilibrium Model for Tax Policy Evaluation.* Chicago: University of Chicago Press, 1985.

Ballard, Charles L., and Steven G. Medema, "The Marginal Efficiency Effects of Taxes and Subsidies in the Presence of Externalities: A Computational General Equilibrium Approach." Unpublished manuscript, Department of Economics, Michigan State University, East Lansing, July 1989.

Ballard, Charles L., John B. Shoven, and John Whalley, "General Equilibrium Computations of the Marginal Welfare Costs of Taxes in the United States," *American Economic Review* 75, no. 1, (March 1985): 128–138.

Barbash, F. "High Court Refuses to Ease Laws on Job Safety, Health," *The Washington Post* (June 18, 1981): A2.

Barbera, Anthony J., and Virginia D. McConnell, "The Impact of Environmental
    Regulations on Industrial Productivity: Direct and Indirect Effects," *Journal of
    Environmental Economics and Management* 18(1) (January 1990): 50–65.

Barker, Terry; Frederick van der Ploeg, and Martin Weale, "A Balanced System of
    National Accounts for the United Kingdom," *Review of Income and Wealth* 30
    (December 1984): 461–485.

Bartel, Ann P., and Lacy Glenn Thomas, "Direct and Indirect Effects of Regulation: A
    New Look at OSHA's Impact," *Journal of Law and Economics* 28, no. 1 (April
    1985): 1–25.

Bartel, Ann P. and Lacy Glenn Thomas, "Predation Through Regulation: The Wage and
    Profit Effects of the Occupational Safety and Health Administration and the
    Environmental Protection Agency," *Journal of Law and Economics* 30, no. 2
    (October 1987): 239–264.

Behr, Peter, "Sinister Side of Benzene Key to Case." *The Washington Post* (July 3, 1980).

Bergman, Lars, "General Equilibrium Effects of Environmental Policy: A CGE-Modeling
    Approach." *Environmental and Resource Economics* 1(1)(1991): 43–61.

Bernheim, B. Douglas, John Karl Scholz, and John B. Shoven, "Consumption Taxation
    in a General Equilibrium Model: How Reliable are Simulation Results?,"
    Unpublished manuscript, Department of Economics, Stanford University, Stanford,
    California, September 1989.

Bick, James H., et al., *Nonfuel Minerals Policy Review: Environmental Quality, Health,
    and Safety*, MTR–79W00088, McLean, Virginia, The MITRE Corporation, February
    1980.

Blackmon, Glenn, and Richard Zeckhauser, "Fragile Commitments and the Regulatory
    Process," *Yale Journal on Regulation* 9, no. 1 (Winter 1992).

Blank, Eric and Stephen Pomerance, "After-the-Fact Regulatory Review: Balancing
    Competing Concerns," *Yale Journal on Regulation* 9, no. 1 (Winter 1992).

Bord, Nancy A. "A Framework for Assessing Analytical Tools in Contemporary Social
    Science," Unpublished paper, Massachusetts Institute of Technology, Cambridge,
    Massachusetts, 1969.

Bord, Nancy A. "Addressing Employment Effects in the Regulatory Review Process"
    Draft final report prepared for the National Commission for Employment Policy,
    September 9, 1992.

Bord, Nancy A. and William G. Laffer III, "George Bush's Hidden Tax: The Explosion
    in Regulation," *Backgrounder* no. 905 (Washington, D.C.: The Heritage
    Foundation, July 10, 1992).

Boyd, Roy, and Uri, Noel, "The Cost of Improving Quality of the Environment," *Journal
    of Policy Modeling* 13(1)(1991): 115–140.

Breger, Marshall J. "Introduction to 'A Symposium on the Supreme Court's Admin-
    istrative Law Docket,'" *The Administrative Law Journal of the American University*
    6, no. 2 (Summer 1992).

Brennan, Kathleen M., and Jerome T. Bentley, *Supporting Analyses for Regulatory
    Impact Analysis of the National Ambient Air Quality Standards for Lead.* Princeton,
    N.J.: Mathtech, Inc., May 1991.

Breyer, Stephen, *Regulation and Its Reform.* Cambridge, Mass.: Harvard University Press,
    1982.

Brooke, Anthony, David Kendrick, and Alexander Meeraus, *GAMS: A User's Guide.*
    Redwood City, California: The Scientific Press, 1988.

Brookshire, David, Ronald G. Cummings, and William Schulze, *Valuing Public Goods: An Assessment of the Contingent Valuation Method.* Totawa, N.J.: Roman & Allenhold, 1986.

Browing, Graeme, "Getting the Last Word," *The National Journal* (September 14, 1991).

Bruff, Harold H., "Presidential Management of Agency Rulemaking," *The George Washington Law Review* 57, no. 3 (January 1989).

Cabbera, Sigfriedo A. "Overregulation Is Strangling U.S. Economy," *Human Events* (April 1992).

Canto, Victor A., Douglas H. Joines, and Arthur B. Laffer, *Foundations of Supply-Side Economics: Theory and Evidence* New York: Academic Press, 1983.

Canto, Victor A., Douglas H. Joines, and Arthur B. Laffer, "Tax Rates, Factor Employment, Market Production, and Welfare," in *Foundations of Supply-Side Economics: Theory and Evidence* edited by Victor A. Canto, Douglas H. Joines, and Arthur B. Laffer, New York: Academic Press, 1983.

Citizens for a Sound Economy Foundation, "Comments on Regulatory Impact Analysis Submitted by EPA for Proposed Title V Operating Permit Regulations," Washington, D.C.: July 1992.

Clark, T. "Carter's Assault on the Costs of Regulation," *National Journal* 10, No. 32, (August 12, 1978): 1284.

Clark, T. "Do the Benefits Justify the Costs? Prove It, Says the Administration," *National Journal* 13, No. 31 (August 18, 1981).

Clark, Timothy, Marvin Kosters, and James C. Miller III, eds., *Reforming Regulation.* Washington, D.C.: American Enterprise Institute, 1980.

Council on Competitiveness, "Reducing the Burden of Government Regulation," Memorandum for Department and Agency Heads, Washington, D.C.: January 28, 1992.

Council on Competitiveness, *Report on Regulation.* Washington, D.C.: February 1992.

Crandall, Robert W. "What Makes Deregulation Happen?" *The American Enterprise* March/April 1992.

Crandall, Robert W. *Why Is the Cost of Environmental Regulation So High?*, Policy Study no. 110, Center for the Study of American Business, Washington University, St. Louis, Missouri, May 1992.

Crandall, Robert W. and John D. Graham, "The Effect of Fuel Economy Standards on Automobile Safety," *Journal of Law and Economics* XXXII (April 1989): 97–118.

Cummings, Ronald G., and Glenn W. Harrison, *Identifying and Measuring Nonuse Values for Natural and Environmental Resources: A Critical Review of the State of the Art.* Washington, D.C.: American Petroleum Institute, 1992a.

Cummings, Ronald G., and Glenn W. Harrison, "Existence Values and Compensable Damages: Judicial Reliance on Empty Economic Concepts?," Economics working paper B–92–5, Division of Research, College of Business Administration, University of South Carolina, Columbia, 1992b.

Cummings, Ronald G., and Glenn W. Harrison, "Was the Ohio Court Well Informed In Their Assessment of the Accuracy of the Contingent Valuation Method?," *Natural Resources Journal* 33 (1993).

*Daily Labor Report*er, "Clinton Signs Regulatory Review Order; Issues Instructions to Agencies, OIRA," (October 1, 1993): A-17–A-19.

Davis, Bob, "What Price Safety?" *The Wall Street Journal* (July 6, 1992).

Davis, Bob, and Bruce Ingersoll, "Clinton's Team Moves to Extend Regulation in Variety of Industries," *The Wall Street Journal* (April 13, 1993).

DeFina, Robert H. "Unions, Relative Wages, and Economic Efficiency," *Journal of Labor Economics* 1 (1983): 408–429.

Denison, Edward F. *Trends in American Economic Growth, 1929–1982*. Washington, D.C.: Brookings Institution, 1985.

Dickens, William T., and Lawrence F. Katz, "Inter-Industry Wage Differences and Industry Characteristics," in *Unemployment and the Structure of Labor Markets* edited by K. Lang and J. S. Leonard. New York: Basil Blackwell, 1987.

Diwan, Ishac, "Discussant's Comments" in *International Trade and the Environment*, edited by P. Low. (Washington, D.C.: The World Bank, Discussion Paper No.159, 1992).

Dixit, Avinash K., and Victor Norman, *Theory of International Trade* Welwyn, United Kingdom: Nisbet, 1980.

Dixit, Avinash K., and Victor Norman, "Gains From Trade Without Lump–Sum Compensation." *Journal of International Economics* 21 (1986): 111–122.

Dixon, Peter B., B. R. Parmenter, John Sutton, and D. P. Vincent, *ORANI: A Multisectoral Model of the Australian Economy*. Amsterdam: North-Holland, 1982.

Donohue, John J. "Is Title VII Efficient?" *University of Pennsylvania Law Review* 134 (1986): 1411.

Donohue, John J. "Further Thoughts on Employment Discrimination Legislation: A Reply to Judge Posner," *University of Pennsylvania Law Review* 136 (1987): 523.

Donohue, John J. "Advocacy versus Analysis in Assessing Employment Discrimination Law: A Review of Richard Epstein's *Forbidden Grounds*," Stanford Law Review (1992).

Ehrenberg, Ronald G. and Robert S. Smith, *Modern Labor Economics: Theory and Public Policy*, 4th ed. New York: HarperCollins, 1991.

Epstein, Richard A. *Forbidden Grounds: The Case Against Employment Discrimination Laws*. Cambridge, Mass.: Harvard University Press, 1992.

Evans, Paul, "Fiscal Policy and the Labor Market," in *Foundations of Supply-Side Economics: Theory and Evidence* edited by Victor A. Canto, Douglas H. Joines, and Arthur B. Laffer, New York: Academic Press, 1983.

Farber, Henry S. "The Analysis of Union Behavior," in *Handbook of Labor Economics*, Volume 2, edited by O. Ashenfelter and R. Layard. Amsterdam: North-Holland, 1986.

Freeman, Richard B. "Individual Mobility and Union Voice in the Labor Market," *American Economic Review* (Papers & Proceedings) 66: (1976) 361–368.

Freeman, Richard B., and James L. Medoff, *What Do Unions Do?* New York: Basic Books, 1984.

Funk, William F. "Hurdles to Justice: Justiciability Issues in the Supreme Court," *The Administrative Law Journal of the American University* 6, no. 2 (Summer 1992).

Gibbons, Robert, and Lawrence Katz, "Does Ability Explain Inter–Industry Wage Differentials?" *Review of Economic Studies* 59, (1992): 515–535.

Gray, Wayne B. "The Cost of Regulation: OSHA, EPA and the Productivity Slowdown," *American Economic Review* 77, no. 5 (December 1987): 998–1006.

Gray, Wayne B. "The Impact of OSHA and EPA Regulation on Productivity Growth," *Journal of Regulation and Social Costs* 1, no. 3 (June 1991): 25–47.

Hahn, Robert W. "Regulation: Past, Present and Future," *Harvard Journal of Law and Public Policy* 13, no. 1 (Winter 1990): 167–228.

Hahn, Robert W. and John A. Hird, "The Costs and Benefits of Regulation: Review and Synthesis," *Yale Journal on Regulation* 8, no. 1 (Winter 1991): 233–278.

Hahn, Robert W. and Thomas D. Hopkins, "Regulation/Deregulation: Looking Backward, Looking Forward," *The American Enterprise* 3, no. 4 (July/August 1992): 70–79.

Hanke, Steve H. and Stephen J. K. Walters, "Social Regulation: A Report Card," *Journal of Regulation and Social Costs* 1, no. 1 (September 1990): 5–34.

Harberger, Arnold C. "Monopoly and Resource Allocation," *American Economic Review* (Papers & Proceedings): 44 (1954): 77–87.

Harberger, Arnold C. "The Measurement of Waste," *American Economic Review* (Papers & Proceedings) 54, (1962a): 58–76.

Harberger, Arnold C. "The Incidence of the Corporation Income Tax," *Journal of Political Economy* 70 (1962b): 215–240.

Harberger, Arnold C. *Taxation and Welfare*. Chicago: University of Chicago Press, 1974.

Harrison, Glenn W. "A General Equilibrium Analysis of Tariff Reductions," in *General Equilibrium Trade Policy Modelling,* edited by T. N. Srinivasan and J. Whalley. Cambridge, Mass.: MIT Press, 1986.

Harrison, Glenn W. "The Sensitivity Analysis of Applied General Equilibrium Models with MPSS: Users Guide." Unpublished manuscript, Department of Economics, University of South Carolina, Columbia, S.C. June 1990.

Harrison, Glenn W., and Larry J. Kimbell, "Economic Interdependence in the Pacific Basin: A General Equilibrium Approach," in *New Developments in Applied General Equilibrium Analysis*, edited by J. Piggott and J. Whalley: Cambridge, United Kingdom: Cambridge University Press, 1985.

Harrison, Glenn W., and Richard J. Manning, "Best Approximate Aggregation of Input-Output Systems," *Journal of the American Statistical Association* 82 (December 1987): 1027–1031.

Harrison, Glenn W., Thomas F. Rutherford, and Ian Wooton, "Economic Impact of The European Community," *American Economic Review* (Papers & Proceedings) 65 (May 1989): 288–294.

Harrison, Glenn W., Thomas F. Rutherford, Ian Wooton, "The Common Agricultural Policy of the European Communities," Working Paper no. 8905, Centre for the Study of International Economic Relations, Department of Economics, University of Western Ontario, 1990 (revised).

Harrison, Glenn W., Thomas F. Rutherford, and Ian Wooton, "An Empirical Database for a General Equilibrium Model of the European Communities," *Empirical Economics* 16 (1991): 95–120.

Harrison, Glenn W., and E. E. Rutström, "The Effect of Manufacturing Sector Protection in Australia and ASEAN: A General Equilibrium Analysis." in *The Political Economy of Manufacturing Protection: Experiences of ASEAN and Australia* edited by C. Findlay and R. Garnaut. Sydney: Allen & Unwin, 1986.

Harrison, Glenn W., and H. D. Vinod, "The Sensitivity Analysis of Applied General Equilibrium Models: Completely Randomized Factorial Sampling Designs." *The Review of Economics and Statistics* 79 (May 1992): 357–362.

Hazilla, Michael and Raymond J. Kopp, "Social Cost of Environmental Quality Regulations: A General Equilibrium Analysis," *Journal of Political Economy* 98, no. 4 (1990): 853–873.

Heckman, James J., and Brook S. Payner, "Determining the Impact of Federal Antidiscrimination Policy on the Economic Status of Blacks: A Study of South Carolina," *American Economic Review* 79 (1989).

Heldman, Dan C., James T. Bennett, and Manuel H. Johnson, *Deregulating Labor Relations*, The Fisher Institute, Dallas, Texas, 1981.

Helwege, Jean, "Sectoral Shifts and Interindustry Wage Differentials," *Journal of Labor Economics* 10 (1992): 55–84.

Higgs, Robert, "The Growth of Government in the United States," *The Freeman* (August 1990).

Hilts, Philip J., "Quayle Council Debate: Issue of Control," *The New York Times* (December 16, 1991): B11.

Hirsch, Barry T., *Labor Unions and the Economic Performance of Firms.* Kalamazoo, Michigan: W. E. Upjohn Institute for Employment Research, 1992.

Hirsch, Barry T., "Firms Investment Behavior and Collective Bargaining Strategy" *Industrial Relations* 31 (1992): 95–121.

Hirsch, Barry T., and John T. Addison, *The Economic Analysis of Unions.* Boston: Allen & Unwin, 1986.

Holman, Frank W., Jr. "Regulatory Reform," in *MAPI Executive Letter* Washington, D.C.: Manufacturers' Alliance for Productivity and Innovation, February 28, 1992.

Hopkins, Thomas D. *Cost of Regulation,* Rochester, New York: Rochester Institute of Technology Public Policy Working Paper, December 1991.

Hopkins, Thomas D. "The Costs of Federal Regulation," *Journal of Regulation and Social Costs* 2, no. 1 (March 1992): 5–31.

ICF Resources Incorporated, *Comparison of the Economic Impacts of the Acid Rain Provisions of the Senate Bill (S.1630) and the House Bill (S.1630)* Washington, D.C.: U.S. EPA, July 1990.

Interagency Regulatory Liaison Group, *Hazardous Substances Summary and Full Development Plan,* Washington, D.C., December 1978.

Interagency Regulatory Liaison Group, *Regulatory Reporter* 1, no. 1, (April 1979): 14.

Ippolito, Richard A. "A Study of the Regulatory Effects of the Employee Retirement Income Security Act," *Journal of Law and Economics* 31, no. 1 (October 1988).

Isaac, Daniel, "They Can't Compete," *Legal Times* (September 7, 1992).

Johansen, Leif, *A Multi-Sectoral Study of Economic Growth.* Amsterdam: North-Holland, 1960.

Johnson, F. Reed, "Income Distributional Effects of Air Pollution Abatement: A General Equilibrium Approach." *Atlantic Economic Journal* 8(4)(1980): 10–21.

Joines, Douglas H. "A Neoclassical Model of Fiscal Policy, Employment, and Capital Accumulation," in *Foundations of Supply-Side Economics: Theory and Evidence* edited by Victor A. Canto, Douglas H. Joines, and Arthur B. Laffer, New York: Academic Press, 1983.

Jones, Ronald W., "A Three-Factor Model in Trade Theory and History," in *Trade, Balance of Payments, and Growth: Papers in Honor of Charles P. Kindleberger* edited by J. Bhagwati et. al. Amsterdam: North-Holland, 1971.

Jones, Ronald W., and Jose A. Schienkman., "The Relevance of the Two-Sector Production Model in Trade Theory." *Journal of Political Economy* 85 (October 1977): 909–1035.

Jorgenson, Dale W., and David T. Slesnick, "Efficiency Versus Equity in Natural Gas Price Regulation," *Journal of Econometrics* 30 (1985): 301–316.

Jorgenson, Dale W. and Peter J. Wilcoxen, "Environmental Regulation and U.S. Economic Growth," Harvard Institute of Economic Research Discussion Paper no. 1458, October 1989.

Jorgenson, Dale W., and Peter J. Wilcoxen, "Environmental Regulation and U.S. Economic Growth." *Rand Journal of Economics,* 21(2) (Summer 1990a): 314–340.

Jorgenson, Dale W., and Peter J. Wilcoxen, "Intertemporal General Equilibrium Modeling of U.S. Environmental Regulation." *Journal of Policy Modeling* 12(4)(1990b): 715–744.

Kahn, Alfred E. "Deregulation: Looking Backward and Looking Forward," *Yale Journal on Regulation* 7, no. 2 (Summer 1990).

Kalaba, Robert, and Leigh Tesfatsion, "Nonlocal Automated Sensitivity Analysis." MRG Working Paper #M8911, Modelling Research Group, Department of Economics, University of Southern California, July 1989.

Katz, Lawrence F. "Efficiency Wage Theories: A Partial Evaluation," in *NBER Macroeconomics Annual 1986* edited by S. Fischer (Cambridge, Mass.: MIT Press, 1986.

Katz, Lawrence F., and Lawrence H. Summers, "Industry Rents: Evidence and Implications," *Brookings Papers on Economic Activity: Microeconomics* (1989): 209–75.

Kazman, Sam, "Deadly Overcaution: FDA's Drug Approval Process," *Journal of Regulation and Social Costs* 1, no. 1 (September 1990): 35–54.

Kendall, M. G., A. Stuart, and J. K. Ord, *The Advanced Theory of Statistics*, Volume 3. London: Griffin, III, 1983).

Kimbell, Larry J., and Glenn W. Harrison, "On The Solution of General Equilibrium Models." *Economic Modelling* 3 (1986): 197–212.

Kneese, Allen V. *Economics and the Environment* (New York: Penguin, 1977).

Kniesner, Thomas J. and John D. Leeth, "Improving Workplace Safety," *Regulation* (Fall 1991).

Kokoski, Mary F., and V. Kerry Smith, "A General Equilibrium Analysis of Partial Equilibrium Welfare Measures: The Case of Climate Change," *American Economic Review* 77 (June 1987): 331–341.

Krueger, Alan B., and Lawrence H. Summers, "Reflections on the Inter-Industry Wage Structure," in *Unemployment and the Structure of Labor Markets* edited by K. Lang and J. S. Leonard. New York: Basil Blackwell, 1987.

Laffer, Arthur B. "Supply-Side Economics," *Financial Analysts Journal* (September/October 1981): 29–43.

Lave, Lester B. "Risky Business: Thinking About the Benefits and Costs of Government Regulation," *The American Enterprise* (November/December 1992).

Leonard, Jonathan S. "Antidiscrimination or Reverse Discrimination: The Impact of Changing Demographics, Title VII, and Affirmative Action on Productivity," *Journal of Human Resources* XIX, no. 2 (Spring 1984): 145–74.

Lilien, David M., "Sectoral Shifts and Cyclical Unemployment," *Journal of Political Economy* 90, (1982): 777–793.

Litan, Robert E. and William D. Nordhaus, *Reforming Federal Regulation.* New Haven, Conn.: Yale University Press, 1983.

Lloyd, Peter J. "Protection Policy and the Assignment Rule," in *Protection and Competition in International Trade* edited by H. Kierzkowski. London: Basil Blackwell, 1987.

Lofting, Everard M., and Davis, H. Craig, "An Interindustry Analysis of Industrial Air Pollutants for the State and Substate Regions of California," Final Report. Sacramento, Calif: State of California Air Resources Board, September 1979.

Low, Patrick, ed., *International Trade and the Environment.* Washington, D.C.: The World Bank, Discussion Paper no. 159, 1992a).

Low, Patrick, "Trade Measures and Environmental Quality: The Implications for Mexico's Exports.," in *International Trade and the Environment* edited by P. Low. Washington, D.C.: The World Bank, Discussion Paper no. 159, 1992b.

Lutter, Randall and John Morrall, "Health-Health Analysis: A New Way to Evaluate Health and Safety Regulation." Unpublished paper, October 1992.

Mackay-Smith, A. "Cotton Dust Ruling Is Expected to Spur Industry Trend Toward Modernization." *The Wall Street Journal* (June 18, 1981): 24.

Maloney, Michael T., Robert E. McCormick, and Robert D. Tollison, "Economic Regulation, Competition, Governments and Specialized Resources," *Journal of Law and Economics* 27, no. 2 (October 1984).

Mathieson, Lars. "Computation of Economic Equilibria by a Sequence of Linear Complementarity Problems." *Mathematical Programming Study* 23 (1985).

McGunty, Thomas O. "Regulatory Analysis and Regulatory Reform," Texas Law Review 65, no. 7 (June 1987).

Melo, Jaime de, and David Tarr, General Equilibrium Analysis of U.S. Foreign Trade Policy. Cambridge, Mass.: MIT Press, 1992.

Miles, Marc A. *Beyond Monetarism: Finding the Road to Stable Money.* New York: Basic Books, 1984.

Miller, James C. III and Philip Mink, "The Ink of the Octopus," *Policy Review* (Summer 1992).

"Minimum Wage: Rate Hike Would Hurt Poor, Study Says," *Employment & Training Reporter* (January 27, 1993): 399–400.

Mohnen, Volker A. "The Challenge of Acid Rain." *Scientific American* 259 (August 1988): 30-38.

Morrall, John F. III, "Controlling Regulatory Costs: The Use of Regulatory Budgeting," Paper Prepared for the Public Management Service of the Organization for Economic Cooperation and Development, Paris, July 1992.

Murphy, Kevin, and Robert H. Topel, "Unemployment, Risk, and Earnings: Testing for Equalizing Wage Differences in the Labor Market," in *Unemployment and the Structure of Labor Markets* edited by K. Lang and J. S. Leonard. New York: Basil Blackwell, 1987a.

Murphy, Kevin, and Robert H. Topel, "The Evolution of Unemployment in the United States: 1968–1985," in *NBER Macroeconomic Annual, 1987* edited by S. Fischer. Cambridge, Mass: MIT Press, 1987b.

Nestor, Deborah Vaughn, and Carl A. Pasurka, "Alternative Specifications for Environmental Control Costs in a General Equilibrium Framework." Unpublished manuscript, Economic Analysis and Research Branch, U.S. Environmental Protection Agency, 1992a.

Nestor, Deborah Vaughn, and Carl A. Pasurka, "Applied General Equilibrium Model for the Analysis of Environmental Protection Activities in the U.S." Unpublished manuscript, Economic Analysis and Research Branch, U.S. Environmental Protection Agency, November 1992b.

Neumark, David. *Employment Effects of Minimum and Subminimum Wages*, Washington, D.C.: Employment Policies Institute, February 1993.

Nguyen, Trien T., Carlo Perroni, and Randall M. Wigle, "A Micro-Consistent Data Set for the Analysis of World Trade: Sources and Methods," Unpublished manuscript, Department of Economics, Wilfrid Laurier University, Waterloo, Ontario. 1991 (revised).

Noll, Roger G. "Regulation after Reagan," *AEI Journal on Government and Society* no. 3 (1988).

Nordheimer, Jon, "Laid–Off Boatyard Workers Rehired," *The New York Times* (August 3, 1993).

Office of Management and Budget, *Regulatory Program of the United States Government: April 1, 1987–March 31, 1988*. Washington, D.C.: U.S. Government Printing Office, May 1987.

Office of Management and Budget, *Regulatory Program of the United States Government: April 1, 1988–March 31, 1989*. Washington, D.C.: U.S. Government Printing Office, May 1988.

Office of Management and Budget, Office of Information and Regulatory Affairs, *Information Collection Review Handbook*. Washington, D.C.: U.S. Government Printing Office, January 1989.

Office of Management and Budget, *Regulatory Program of the United States Government: April 1, 1991–March 31, 1992*. Washington, D.C.: U.S. Government Printing Office, May 1991).

"OSHA and Work-Place Hazards: Cotton Dust." *Regulation*, 1, No. 2 (July/August 1977): 6.

Olson, Theodore B. "Separation of Powers and the Supreme Court," *The Administrative Law Journal of the American University* 6, no. 2 (Summer 1992).

OMB Watch, *Through the Corridors of Power*. Washington, D.C., 1987.

O'Neill, June E. and David M. O'Neill, "The Impact of a Health Insurance Mandate on Labor Costs and Employment, Empirical Evidence," Washington, D.C.: Employment Policies Institute. September 1993.

Oswald, Andrew J. "The Economic Theory of Trade Unions: An Introductory Survey," *Scandinavian Journal of Economics* 87 (1985): 160–193.

Pagan, Adrian R., and John H. Shannon, "Sensitivity Analysis for Linearized Computable General Equilibrium Models," in *New Developments in Applied General Equilibrium Analysis* edited by J. Piggott and J. Whalley. Cambridge: Cambridge University Press, 1985.

Pagan, Adrian R., and John E. Shannon, "How Reliable Are ORANI Conclusions?" *Economic Record* 63 (March 1987): 33–45.

Pashigan, Peter, "Environmental Regulation: Whose Self--Interests Are Being Protected?" *Economic Inquiry* 23 (1985): 551–584.

Passell, Peter, "Economic Scene: Does raising the minimum wage still mean fewer jobs?" *The New York Times* (February 18, 1993): D2.

Peltzman, Sam, "An Evaluation of Consumer Protection Legislation: The 1962 Drug Amendments," *Journal of Political Economy* (September 1973): 1049–1091.

Pencavel, John H. "Wages, Specific Training, and Labor Turnover in U.S. Manufacturing Industries," *International Economic Review* 13 (1972): 53–64.

Penn & Schoen Associates, Inc., *National Public Opinion Survey on Regulatory Reform*, March 30, 1992.

Perroni, Carlo, and Thomas F. Rutherford, "Regularly Flexible Functional Forms for Applied General Equilibrium Analysis." Unpublished manuscript, Department of Economics, University of Western Ontario, 1989.

Posner, Richard A., "The Efficiency and Efficacy of Title VII," *University of Pennsylvania Law Review* 136 (1987): pp. 513–22.

Press, William H., Brian P. Flannery, Saul Teukolsky, and William T. Vetterling, *Numerical Recipes: The Art of Scientific Computing.* Cambridge: Cambridge University Press, 1986.

Pritzker, David M. "Working Together for Better Regulations," *Natural Resources and the Environment* 5, no. 2 (Fall 1990).

Pritzker, David M. "Administrative Conference Roundtable on Reg-Neg," *Administrative Law News* 17, no. 2 (Winter 1992).

Rauch, Jonathan, "The Regulatory President." *National Journal* 23, no. 48 (November 30, 1991): 2902–2906.

Reinert, Kenneth A., and David W. Roland-Holst, "Social Accounting Matrices and Exogenous Parameter Estimates for U.S. Trade Policy Analysis." Unpublished manuscript, Office of Economics, U.S. International Trade Commission, May 1990.

Reinert, Kenneth A., and David W. Roland-Holst, "Parameter Estimates for U.S. Trade Policy Analysis." Unpublished manuscript, Office of Economics, U.S. International Trade Commission, April 1991.

Reinert, Kenneth A., and David W. Roland-Holst, "A Detailed Social Accounting Matrix for the USA, 1988." *Economic Systems Research* 4(2)(1992): 173–187.

Reinert, Kenneth A., and Clinton R. Shiells, "Trade Substitution Elasticities for Analysis of a North American Free Trade Area." Unpublished manuscript, Office of Economics, U.S. International Trade Commission, January 1991.

Romer, Paul M. "Endogenous Technical Change," *Journal of Political Economy* 98, no. 5, Part 2 (October 1990): S71–S102.

Rubin, Paul H. "The Economics of Regulatory Deception," *Cato Journal* 10, no. 3 (Winter 1991).

Rutherford, Thomas F. "General Equilibrium Modelling With MPS/GE." Unpublished monograph, Department of Economics, University of Western Ontario, April 1989.

Rutherford, Thomas F., and Stanley L. Winer, "Endogenous Policy in a Computational General Equilibrium Framework." Unpublished manuscript, Department of Economics, University of Western Ontario, 1991.

Rutström, E. E. *The Political Economy of Indonesian Protectionism: A General Equilibrium Analysis.* Stockholm: Stockholm School of Economics, 1991.

Rutström, E. E. "Friends, Enemies and Rent-Seeking: Who Protects Whom in Indonesia?" Economics working paper, Division of Research, College of Business Administration, University of South Carolina, Columbia, 1992.

St. Hilaire, France, and John Whalley, "A Microconsistent Equilibrium Data Set for Canada for Use in Tax Policy Analysis." *Review of Income and Wealth* 29 (1983): 175–204.

Sargentich, Thomas O. "The Scope of Judicial Review of Issues of Law: *Chevron Revisited,*" *The Administrative Law Journal of the American University* 6, no. 2 (Summer 1992).

Scholz, John T. "Cooperative Regulatory Enforcement and the Politics of Administrative Effectiveness," *American Political Science Review* 85, no. 1 (March 1991).

Shoven, John B. "The Incidence and Efficiency Effects of Taxes on Income from Capital." *Journal of Political Economy* 84 (1976): 1261–1283.

Shoven John B., and John Whalley, "Applied General Equilibrium Models of Taxation and International Trade: An Introduction and Survey." *Journal of Economic Literature* 22 (1984): 1007–1051.

Shoven, John B., and John Whalley, *Applying General Equilibrium*. New York: Cambridge University Press, 1992.

State of California Department of Water Resources, *Measuring Economic Impacts*. Sacramento, Calif.: Department of Water Resources, Bulletin #210, March 1980.

Stelzer, Irwin M. "Two Styles of Regulatory Reform," *The American Enterprise* (March/April 1990).

Stone, J.R.N., D. G. Champernowne, and J. E. Meade, "The Precision of National Income Estimates." Review of Economic Studies 9(2)(1942): 111–125.

Stuart, Charles E. "Welfare Costs per Dollar of Additional Tax Revenue in the United States." *American Economic Review* 74 (June 1984): 352–362.

Taylor, Lowell J. "The Employment Effects in Retail Trade of a Minimum Wage, Evidence from California," Washington, D.C.: Employment Policies Institute, June 1993.

van Tongeren, Jan W. "Development of an Algorithm for the Compilation of National Accounts And Related Systems of Statistics," *Review of Income and Wealth* 32 (March 1986): 25–47.

U.S. Department of Commerce, *Manufacturer's Pollution Abatement Capital Expenditures and Operating Costs, 1988*, Washington, D.C.: Bureau of the Census, Report MA200(88)–1, September 1988.

U.S. Department of Health and Human Services, *Handbook on Regulatory Impact Analysis and Regulatory Flexibility Analysis in the Department of Health and Human Services*, Washington, D.C.: February 1984.

U.S. Department of Health and Human Services, "Compliance with Executive Orders on the Family and on Federalism," Memorandum to Heads of Operating Divisions and Staff Divisions, Washington, D.C.: March 1988.

U.S. Department of Labor, Occupational Safety and Health Administration, "Occupational Exposure to Cadmium: Final Rules," *Federal Register* (September 14, 1992).

U.S. Department of the Treasury, "U.S. Department of the Treasury Regulatory Burden Reductions," *Treasury News*, (October 20, 1992).

U.S. Environmental Protection Agency, *Regulatory Impact Analysis on the National Ambient Air Quality Standards for Sulphur Oxides (Sulfur Dioxide)* Washington, D.C.: Air Quality Management Division, U.S. EPA, March 1988.

U.S. General Accounting Office, *Letter Report GGD–78–116*, Washington, D.C.

U.S. General Accounting Office, *Risk-Risk Analysis: OMB's Review of a Proposed OSHA Rule*, Washington, D.C.: GAO/PEMD–92–33, July 1992.

U.S. General Accounting Office, *Regulatory Reform: Information on Costs, Cost-Effectiveness, and Mandated Deadlines for Regulations*, Washington, D.C.: GAO/PEMD–95–18BR, March 1995.

U.S. House of Representatives, Committee on Energy and Commerce, "Presidential Control of Agency Rulemaking, An Analysis of Constitutional Issues That May Be Raised by Executive Order 12291." Washington, D.C., June 15, 1981.

U.S. House of Representatives, Committee on Energy and Commerce, "Role of OMB in Regulation." Hearing before the Subcommittee on Oversight and Investigations, Washington, D.C., June 18, 1981.

U.S. Senate, Committee on Governmental Affairs, "Study on Federal Regulation." Volumes I–VI, Washington, D.C., December 1978.

U.S. Senate, Committee on Governmental Affairs, *Regulatory Review Sunshine Act: Report to Accompany S. 1942.* (February 1992).

U.S. Trade Representative, *Review of U.S.-Mexico Environmental Issues.* Washington, D.C.: Office of the U.S. Trade Representative, February 1992.

Van Grasstek, Craig, "The Political Economy of Trade and the Environment in the United States Senate" in *International Trade and the Environment* edited by P. Low. Washington, D.C.: The World Bank, Discussion Paper no. 159, 1992.

Warren, Melinda and James Lis, *Regulatory Standstill: Analysis of the 1993 Federal Regulatory Budget*, Occasional Paper 105, St. Louis: Center for the Study of American Business, Washington University, May 1992.

Washington Institute for Policy Studies, "Regulatory Relief, Regulatory Reform." Washington: Washington Institute for Policy Studies (Bellevue, 1987).

Weidenbaum, Murray L. *The Future of Business Regulation: Private Action and Public Demand.* New York: AMACOM (a division of the American Management Association): 1980.

Weidenbaum, Murray L. *The New Wave of Business Regulation,* Contemporary Issues Series no. 40, St. Louis: Center for the Study of American Business, Washington University, May 1992.

Whalley, John, "How Reliable Is Partial Equilibrium?," *Review of Economics and Statistics* 57 (August 1975): 299–310.

Whalley, John, *Trade Liberalization Among Major World Trading Areas.* Cambridge, Mass.: MIT Press, 1985.

Wheeler, David, and Paul Martin, "Prices, Policies, and the International Diffusion of Clean Technology: The Case of Wood Pulp Production," in *International Trade and the Environment* edited by P. Low. Washington, D.C.: The World Bank, Discussion Paper no. 159, 1992.

Wigle, Randall, "General Equilibrium Evaluation of Canada-U.S. Free Trade Liberalization in a Global Context." *Canadian Journal of Economics* 21 (August 1988): 539–64.

Wigle, Randall, "The Pagan-Shannon Approximation: Unconditional Systematic Sensitivity in Minutes." *Empirical Economics* 16(1)(1991): 35–49.

Wojick, David, "Chaos Theory and Compliance Planning," *Compliance Strategies Review* (October 26, 1992).

Wood, B. Dan and Richard W. Waterman, "The Dynamics of Political Control of the Bureaucracy," *American Political Science Review* 85, no. 3, (September 1991).

Xiao, Baichun, and Patrick Harker, "The Stochastic Linear Complementarity Problem." Decision Sciences Working Paper 88–05, Decision Sciences Department, University of Pennsylvania, Philadelphia, May 1988.

Index

About the Author

NEAL S. ZANK is a consultant and Research Associate at the Center for Global Management and Research at George Washington University. He is co-author of *Reforming Financial Systems: Policy Change and Privatization* (Greenwood, 1991) and *Welfare System Reform: Coordinating Federal, State, and Local Public Assistance Programs* (Greenwood, 1993), and has written numerous articles on job training, foreign aid, and international economic issues. Mr. Zank was Associate Director of the National Commission for Employment Policy (1990–1993), and a staff member for two Presidential commissions and the U.S. Agency for International Development.